A MID-CENTURY AWAKENING

(Testimony of a Time)

A Memoir
by
DOUG MILLER

iUniverse, Inc.
Bloomington

A Mid-Century Awakening
(Testimony of a Time)

iUniverse books may be ordered through booksellers or by contacting:

iUniverse
1663 Liberty Drive
Bloomington, IN 47403
www.iuniverse.com
1-800-Authors (1-800-288-4677)

Cover photograph. From left: Mike Davis, Doug Miller, Jimmy Walker.
Photo taken by Eleanor Wassom, circa Easter, 1957.

ISBN: 978-1-4759-6377-9 (sc)
ISBN: 978-1-4759-6378-6 (ebk)

Library of Congress Control Number: 2012923209

Printed in the United States of America

iUniverse rev. date: 12/26/2012

Dedication

To the Putnam City Class of 1958;
and to David McCasland (Class of 1961).
You wanted the book, Dave. Well, here it is.

FOREWORD

Doug Miller is the only person who could write this book, and I'm so glad he did. It's a book I've been waiting 50 years to read. Along with scores of high school classmates, I'm a beneficiary of Doug's journey to faith. When he finally said "yes" to God, it wasn't a one and done event. Today, ripples from the Rock of Ages dropping into our Oklahoma City high school during the late 1950s continue to pulse outward into the lives of people two generations later.

Doug's authentic, humorous and sometimes gut-wrenching narrative evokes memories of what were touted as "the happiest days of our lives," but really weren't. Did we have fun? Of course! Did we cry when no one was looking? If we were able. The stiff upper lip we inherited from our World War II parents was a noble characteristic, but often functioned as a cork in our emotional bottle rather than a conduit to healing.

When you read about the "high school prayer meeting" phenomenon, try to picture it happening today. I believe it could, and many hope it would. For us, it was simply wild and free, because that's what happens when our hearts wake up and discover the One who made us and why we're here.

David McCasland
Putnam City High School, Class of 1961

INTRODUCTION

In early 1957 I began to live through an experience that I have been analyzing ever since. I did not fully comprehend it while it was going on, and I'm not sure I do even now. At the time I saw myself as a leader of men, shaping and molding and changing lives. My references were all subjective, thus my view of the experience was totally egocentric. But I wouldn't have said that back then. I would have attributed everything that went on, correctly, to the Lord. In fact, I did so many times. But failing to grasp even a particle of the Lord's nature, His purposes, His methods of operation, I was correct for all the wrong reasons. And failing to see myself as I really am—weak, fickle, ignorant, innately selfish—I lost no time in falling into any number of errors from which I could not extricate myself. The experience whirled on by, leaving me to wonder what it all meant.

I have observed that the most profound experiences come and go so softly, barely noticed until they have slipped away. I have also observed that those experiences that roar down on one with great and spectacular accompaniment have the least power to affect long term change. But I doubt that most sixteen year olds know this. On a warm evening in late February, 1957, when I was sixteen, I went into a building. When I came out, barely an hour later, life would never be the same for me. But the life-transforming event had come and gone so quickly that I (basically a seeker of cheap kicks) hardly knew what had happened. The Spirit of God, moving like a gentle breeze, had breathed into my nostrils the breath of life, and I had become a living soul.

This is the story of my salvation, and not of mine only, but of others as well. It is the story of a mid-century awakening in Middle

America among a group of middle-class teenagers. Kids gone mad for Elvis Presley, James Dean, and Buddy Holly, who lived for hotrods and football, found themselves drawn irresistibly to a new Lord, Jesus Christ, who claimed them spirit, soul, and body. Not one of them planned it or would have believed it possible. Some tried to fight it. Others would later deny it.

One of many questions I have asked myself is, why? Why this group and not another? Why this time and this place? Why in just this way? Why not again and again to many others in many places, in many times? I can only answer as the Apostle Paul did centuries ago: "O the depth of the riches both of the wisdom and knowledge of God! How unsearchable are His judgments, and His ways past finding out."

Some might think me parochial or self-serving to write in so personal a way of such an experience. Who, after all, should be interested? Bookshelves abound with the reflections of famous people who, one would assume, have a ready-made audience, whereas I am an unknown. But certain eternal truths, common to all men in all places and times, can be abstracted from an otherwise narrow personal happening. Something which so affected me must strike responsive chords in someone else. This is why I dare to hope that there are those who can identify with an ordinary boy and his ordinary friends, shuffling along from cradle to grave and not particular about how they get there. There must be those who will respond to the story of the Lord's dealings with average people. And maybe some will gain through my story certain insights into experiences they have lived through, or may be living through even now, or may live through yet.

Finally, I must confess that this is a story of human failure. Now this is not a popular topic, for we all like to think of ourselves as successful, or at least we aspire to success. This is why "how-to" books become bestsellers. *How to Gain Victory through Prayer. How to Find Peace Through Bible Memorization. How to be a Spiritual Giant Without Really Trying.* So my imaginary list of titles goes.

I feel compelled to tell the truth. I have been a failure, as have most of the people I know or can read about. Adam failed. Noah failed. Abraham failed and in so doing peopled the earth with those who have been the most persistent enemies of God's chosen people. Israel failed. Christ's Church down across the ages has failed and failed and failed again. The path of the race of man is littered with failure and defeat in most any spiritual enterprise one wishes to name.

My story is not, then, the story of victory but rather the story of how God, in His grace and mercy, can save a man, can carry and keep that man, and can present him faultless before His Throne in that great coming day.

I intend to tell this story as directly as I am able, employing the first person singular. I will tell it as accurately as I can. I have changed some names, however, and created both composite characters and, in some instances, composite situations. I have taken the liberty of leaving some people unnamed if what I have to say about them is uncomplimentary. But I hope to avoid being overly critical of any man or institution. I come to praise the Lord, not to defame man.

I

IN THE BEGINNING, GOD CREATED . . .

1

Well it's one for the money,
Two for the show,
Three to get ready,
Now go, cat, go . . .
~ Carl Perkins ~

Years I spent in vanity and pride,
Caring not my Lord was crucified,
Knowing not it was for me He died,
On Calvary.
~ William R. Newell ~

All stories must begin somewhere, so this one will begin on a raw, overcast day in January 1956. A stiff north wind was whistling down from Saskatchewan, for all I know. I was in a car, moving west on Thirty-Ninth Street Expressway in Oklahoma City. I don't remember where I had been or who I was with. I do know that I wasn't driving, because I was only fifteen, and as yet unlicensed.

From my present vantage point the mid-fifties look beautiful and uncomplicated, though that probably has something to do with my relative ignorance of sub-surface events. The Nazis were done for, Korea over, American military might unchallenged. General MacArthur had returned home to a hero's welcome. Truman, who had fired him, was mentioned in the same breath with Judas and Benedict Arnold. Tail-gunner Joe McCarthy had hunted behind the final bush for his final communist and headed toward his final roundup. The Russians had the bomb, but Alger Hiss got what he had coming, and the same guys who convicted Hiss presided over the Rosenbergs' execution. Gary Cooper gunned down Frank Miller at high noon on a movie set. Frank Miller had probably been a communist. In the White House Eisenhower governed beatifically over our great American nation, aided by a young gut-fighter named Nixon, and all good Republicans sang of peace and prosperity to any who would listen. The peace was more apparent than real. Within the decade Little Rock would erupt in racial violence. Within ten years American cities would be burning, and youth would be in rebellion. Vietnam would be blazing and roaring.

I knew little of this, zipping along Thirty-Ninth Expressway in January of 1956.

Edgar Rice Burroughs was dead. Al Jolson was dead. William Randolph Hearst was dead. Enrico Fermi was dead. Theda Bara was dead. Dale Carnegie was dead. Einstein was dead. Lots of people were dead. But lots were still alive. Elvis Presley waited in the wings. Rock and roll, as performed by Bill Haley and Chuck Berry, and a thousand lesser lights, had taken the country by storm. Preachers denounced it from the nation's pulpits.

Blue jeans and loafers were in. Black and pink were the hip colors. Girls wore large skirts with petticoats. Boys sported crew cuts, or grew their hair long, greased it, and slicked it back on the sides in a style known as the ducktail.

The Yankees and the Dodgers were at each other's throats in almost every World Series. Hogan and Sneed reigned in golf, Kramer and Gonzales in tennis. And Marciano retired from the prize ring, undefeated as the world's heavyweight champion.

Thus the world spread out around me, a sophomore in high school and a football player, tooling down an Oklahoma City freeway on a cold day. My companion (whoever it was) and I had the radio tuned to KOCY, a local rock station, and roaring full-blast. A five minute newsbreak interrupted the lovely noise, but I paid it little attention until the newscaster said something like, "And this just in . . ." What followed got hold of me and wouldn't let go, turning this random excursion into what became, for me, an epic journey.

"Five young missionaries are missing in eastern Ecuador near the headwaters of the Amazon river. It is feared that they have been killed by Indians in that area, and several governments, including our own, are sending in armed parties to try to find them."

Teletypes clicked away in the background.

Later I would read and re-read the account of those five young men, how they had died attempting to get the Gospel of Jesus Christ to a tribe of stone age Ecuadorian Indians called Aucas. I would become acquainted with people who had known these missionaries. I would grow, to a degree, to understand why they had turned their backs on all I prized so dearly to yield up their lives in a distant, nameless jungle. Just then, I only listened and stared out the car's window at the gray world whipping by, bewildered by the idea of men dying for a Jesus I knew only as a symbol of goodness at best, a character in dust-covered books at worst. But I also struggled with a curious longing, a deep desire to share whatever had possessed the missionaries and driven them on. I didn't discuss my feelings with the person driving the car, or with anyone else. Who would have understood when I didn't understand myself? Besides, I always felt sort of weird talking about religion, particularly since I was a football player, and was obliged to project an image of toughness and self-control.

I didn't know it, nor did my family or my best friends, but I had entered a spiritual crisis that would culminate in an experience Christians across the centuries have called rebirth. I'll have more to say about rebirth later, but there is this to say now. I have talked to hundreds of people who have been spiritually reborn, and I have read accounts left by many others. I put it down as an immutable, incontrovertible law that rebirth is preceded by a spiritual crisis of some sort, though the individual may not clearly see it as such while passing through it.

There is a simple reason for this. Rebirth takes place when one not only sees Jesus Christ as a living Savior but casts himself wholly on Him as the only hope for salvation. But one will never do this without first being brought to an understanding of his lost condition. If I am not lost, then I don't need a savior. All unsaved people are lost, of course, but few realize it, so they go on rejecting the One who wishes to save them. Their resistance makes a spiritual crisis necessary. "Whom the Lord would save, He first damns," said Martin Luther. So to anyone living through such an experience I say, lift your head and look up; your redemption draws nigh.

The Father doesn't place His royal robes over a beggar's dress, nor does He fill old wineskins with new wine. He strips naked, cleans down to bedrock, renews, re-creates. He never patched up an old wreck, or whitewashed a dung heap, or put shoddy workmanship on display before His universe. When He does something, He does it right.

But I digress.

I was discussing my spiritual crisis, and how it was heightened by the news of five young missionaries slain in the jungles of Ecuador.

2

Gonna tell Aunt Mary
About Uncle John.
He say he's got the mis'ry,
But he's havin' lotta fun.
~ Little Richard ~

Long my imprisoned spirit lay,
Close-bound in sin and death's dark night.
~ Charles Wesley ~

An individual may be living high, be miserable within, and retain the ability to function brilliantly, particularly when he is a member of a society that rewards outward success and puts little premium on off-beat religious problems. I handled just such a situation fairly well. But I think I would have been much less apt to play the carefree teenager if I had known that many of my closest friends were caught up in a spiritual crisis no less profound and troubling than my own. The Lord was about to shake my high school in particular, and Oklahoma City in general, to the foundations, which means He was preparing other hearts, even as mine, to receive the good news about His Son. But I fancied my situation unique, so I kept it to myself. It came as a great surprise to many when I later explained how unhappy I had been during this period of outward prosperity.

I have said a good deal about my spiritual crisis. I suppose I ought to have a go at describing it. It began when I was fourteen with the death of a second cousin whom, to my knowledge, I had never met. I also had never seen a dead human until I attended his funeral. As I filed past the open coffin, organ music droned in the background, and sunlight streaked through stained glass windows. The too-sweet odor of flowers hung over the room like a pall. Women sniffed into handkerchiefs, and people kept babbling about how natural he looked, just as if he was sleeping. They may have convinced themselves, but they didn't even come close to convincing me. He didn't look at all like a man asleep. He looked stiff and painted and waxen, and above all he looked as dead as a hammer. Something vital had been removed, and that thing in the coffin gave me the creeps. Two women sang, "In the Garden." A preacher mumbled the usual platitudes.

What really troubled me however was that I saw in that coffin my own inescapable end. I know this has to sound trite and maudlin, but it really is true. I couldn't shake the notion that the form in the coffin had once been alive and well, as alert and self-conscious as any fifteen-year-old football player. He had been possessed of emotions, had cared for himself and others, had remembered the past and awaited the future—a future which for him had ceased to exist.

Or had it?

Where I went to church they taught that you never actually died, not in the sense of ceasing to be. Your body could die and rot in the earth, but you, the real, essential you, went on and on, alive and conscious, forever and ever. That could be good, or it could be not so good, because you could go on and on in one of two places. You could go on and on in a very good place called heaven, somewhere way up there; or, you could find yourself faced with the undesirable prospect of going on and on in hell, a frightful inferno somewhere down there. If you were a good guy, which involved behaving in a lot of vaguely Boy Scout type ways, God admitted you to heaven. If you were a consistent louse, you went to hell. Of course, most of the people I admired and emulated were not the types I could imagine in heaven, whereas those I imagined populating heaven didn't excite much admiration in me. Whiskey-swilling, two-fisted he-men were more to my liking.

My infantile theological concepts, gleaned partly from church and partly from the Bible-belt society in which I'd been raised, did nothing to assuage the rising fear of my own imminent demise. Someday I would be the one in the silk-lined box. What then? I believe I had a notion that somewhere in the universe, beneath the all-seeing eye of a God who never slept, a giant scale teetered in the inter-galactic winds, and upon one's death his good deeds would be weighed on the scale against his bad ones. If the scale tilted in the wrong direction, eternal troubled loomed. So I'd better be a good Boy Scout and pile up all the good deeds I could. I would need them one of these days.

I'm sure that my behavior improved slightly for a while after the funeral. But I could never sustain such effort. Why should I drag myself uphill against the grain of my deepest nature when I could lay back, relax and slide down the great roller coaster of life? I know that the shock of my first funeral wore off quickly, but I also know that it became impossible for me to think about God without feeling uncomfortable and guilty.

So began my spiritual crisis, my initial confrontation with the God Who had thundered from Sinai, "The soul that sinneth, it shall die." How he longed to be righteous, this incorrigible sinner! And how he struggled against the very idea of righteousness, embodied, as he saw it, in mousy weirdoes and stained-glass saints.

Within a year I saw another friend buried, not an old cousin I had never met, but a basketball player my own age named Rusty Borden. One evening he and a friend were fishing below the damn at Lake Overholser. He had waded into the river for a cast. A thunderstorm came up, and in as much time as it took lightning to strike, Rusty Borden was no longer among the living. For him, time for good resolutions had run out. I lay in bed that night, unable to sleep, rain drumming on the roof above me, wondering when my time would come.

Once again, I feel that anyone reading this is apt to feel that I'm being melodramatic and phony. Just the opposite is true. I'm actually understating the case because I can't muster up the language to describe the maelstrom that had swept me up and threatened to suck me under. If Rusty Borden could be snatched away in the prime of life, who could guarantee my safety from one moment to the next? I had to get my life straightened out so that I could stand unafraid before God and say, "I'm ready when you are." So I turned to the only source of comfort I knew—religion.

Now most folks I knew had a religion of some sort and acknowledged a Supreme Being of one kind or another. And with regard to approaching this Supreme Being, they usually went through a prescribed ritual of organized posturing and chanting, and this was their *religion*. I was a baptized communicant in one of the old-line Protestant denominations, and while we tolerated others fairly well, we smugly suspected that we stood a bit closer to the true center of activity than they. I had gone to church all of my life on a fairly regular basis, and I had correctly imbibed, as far as I could tell, about as much holiness as anyone else. Further, I took my religion about as seriously as the next guy, or at least I thought I did until my encounters with death convinced me I had failed to grasp something.

I understood that the God of the Bible was called Father, and that we were His children. Of course, Jesus was His only begotten Son, but I was His son too. That didn't make a great deal of sense, but I would worry about that later. Someone said Jesus died for me and that this death had occurred over 1,900 years prior to my existence, all of which made even less sense than the Father-Son business.

Ah, me . . .

But on to more pressing problems. I had to whip my life into shape so that God would like me. That's nothing to worry about, someone assured me, because God loves everybody. *Well*, I thought, *maybe He does, but if so why am I toting around this enormous burden of guilt?*

Of all the treadmills one can get on, none is so maddening and futile as the one marked, "Religion." It consumes all your efforts, energies and passions and then leaves you as lost as when you began. You try to be good, but you fail to be even moderately decent. You try to pray, but you get no further than mouthing words someone else wrote centuries before. You read the Bible looking for comfort, but if you understand a word of it, you find more condemnation heaped upon you. You want to believe, and you try to work up a living faith (because you heard someone quoting John 3:16), but the whole thing strains the credulity of an honest person. So you wind up involved in semi-exalted make believe. You need a vital relationship with a Living Savior, but you are forced back, again and again, into the living prison of yourself, with the resolution that, okay, you bungled it that time but you'll try harder tomorrow. This was the spiritual crisis plaguing me on the cold day in January when I heard that the five missionaries had died in Ecuador. In the well-known and oft-quoted words of Chester A. Riley: "What a revolting development this is!"

3

Well you may go to college,
You may go to school,
You may drive a pink Cadillac,
But don't you be nobody's fool.
~ Elvis Presley ~

I am seriously waiting
for Billy Graham and Elvis Presley
to change roles seriously.
~ Lawrence Ferlinghetti ~

The intersection of 23rd and MacArthur streets looked different in the summer of 1956 from what one sees there now. Today a shopping center covers the southeast corner, but back then it was occupied by a drive-in joint that sold malts for a quarter, hamburgers for a quarter, and Cokes for a dime. There wasn't much room inside, but that didn't matter because few went in there anyway. The parking lot around the building was spacious, and carhops flitted from car to car. Music from the jukebox inside issued forth from large speakers hung in brackets on each side of the building. Drop a coin into the slot. Push B-23. Buddy Knox sings, "All I want is a party doll," and those citizens passing along 23rd Street get the benefit of his singing whether or not they want it. Every high school has a hangout. This was ours.

You cruised through the lot in your car, assuming you owned one, and pulled in beside a car full of girls. Hi, honey, where ya been all my life, etc. etc.. Many interesting boy-girl relationships began at the old drive-in to the pulsing rhythm of rock-and-roll music. Many others broke off there, with tears and returned rings. Sometimes warring factions met and fists flew, but there was an amazing paucity of bloodshed considering the emotion-charged atmosphere.

I first heard the name Elvis Presley at the drive-in in the summer of 1956. "So what?" I hear someone whisper. "You begin by saying you intend to tell us about your salvation, then you go rambling off into a discussion about Elvis Presley. Perhaps this book should be called, '*Confessions of a Repentant Rock Freak.*'"

But Presley, you see, was important. I can't even think of the 50s without him.

Jerry Shipley and I climbed into his father's Buick one summer evening and drove five miles to a record store near Oklahoma City University to buy a 45 rpm recording that had been cut in a rundown dump on Union Avenue in Memphis. It was on the Sun recording label. The singer: Elvis Presley. The song: "Mystery Train." We took the record home and played it over and over. "Train I ride," the singer wailed out at us, "fifteen coaches long . . ."

Presley became the overnight spokesman for our generation, bumping and grinding, sneering and defying authority, calling down upon himself the anathemas of clergy and educators, horrifying some parents and puzzling others.

"Listen to me, baby," he sang, "what I'm talking about. Come on back to me, little girl, so we can play some house . . ." Then he wiggled his hips, and females screamed all across the Republic.

"I've been trav'lin' night 'n day, I've been runnin' all the way, baby, tryin' to get to you . . ." And he stood sort of stiff-legged and quivered below the knees, and thousands of women lost consciousness and were hauled on stretchers out of the nation's auditoriums.

The older generation agreed that, whatever else might be said about the man, the bottom line was that he was a rotten singer. What he did wasn't music at all; it was a bunch of unintelligible screaming with all those vulgar gyrations mixed in. But Presley's very inability to communicate with the older folks made him all the more attractive to us. They could have Como and Sinatra. Elvis was ours.

Quicker, nearly, than I can tell of it, Elvis Presley took charge of the civilized world, and it went screaming mad. I saw all this. The summer raced on. I was not saved.

At the peak of this scarcely-controlled insanity, Billy Graham hit town to hold a series of meetings. He set up at the state fairgrounds, pressed the local churches into service, got himself a multi-denominational choir, which Cliff Barrows taught to sing "How Great Thou Art" and the first fourteen verses of "Just as I am," and he commenced to preach the Gospel.

He irritated me no end.

I was trying to play baseball on an American Legion team that summer. We played on a diamond just south of the fairgrounds, and the singing carried down loud and clear to my position in center field. Something inside me whispered that I should be up there where Billy was preaching, but instead of obeying this inner voice, I made fun of the singers and of the entire affair. Odd, isn't it, the darkness and rebelliousness of the human heart? I wouldn't dare be caught in Billy's meetings, so it took others, months after the fact, to tell me of what had gone on night after night, thirty nights in all, at the Oklahoma State Fairgrounds.

He stood on a podium. There were no electrified instruments, no gaudy lights, nothing to appeal to man's natural desire for the sensational. Above him, brilliant with stars, stretched the enormous skies of summer. The wind blew through his hair, ruffled the pages of his well-thumbed Bible. At his feet, spreading back and across the infield of the stadium, a mass of upturned faces awaited his opening salvo.

They had come for miles to sit on this infield, at this place and in this time, and to hear a man with a message. Grandmothers were there, fanning themselves with cardboard fans from funeral homes. Churches had come in delegations. Some people wandered in out of curiosity, while others were dragged along by nagging spouses.

They waited. Silence settled down like a curtain, and only the wind moved with complete freedom.

He seemed very young, very alone and vulnerable. All had withdrawn from him.

"John," he said, "the third chaptah, the sixteenth verse. John, the third chaptah, the sixteenth verse. For God—so loved the world—that He gave—He gave—He gave His only begotten Son . . ." His voiced rolled in waves across the crowd. "That whosoever . . . That whosoever means you. It means you. It means you and you . . ." He jabbed his finger, rapier-like, at the crowd.

Individuals later reported that they had felt they were there alone, and that Graham spoke directly to them, that this anachronistic throwback to the prophets of Israel had singled them out and skewered them with the razor-sharp sword of Jehovah. Words like sin, hell and judgment smote their hearts with the force of a nine pound hammer.

"You may be a church membah, you may not be a membah of any church. But without Christ, I don't ca'ah who you are or what you are, you'll nevah be in heaven."

But it was so corny and hick and hopelessly down-home-ish. Revival meetings were things of the past—for rural types and tenant farmers, and for people in overalls and brogans. Was it really true, people asked one another, that this young man had brought Los Angeles to its knees and set the city slickers on the sawdust trail?

"I'm going to ask hundreds of you to do something very difficult. I'm going to ask you to get up and come and stand here, and by coming you say, 'I receive Jesus Christ as my Lord and Savior.' I know it's a long way from the back row, but Jesus went a long way to the cross for you . . ."

Just as I am, without one plea,
But that Thy blood was shed for me,
And that Thou bidst me come to Thee,
Oh, Lamb of God, I come . . .

And they came by the hundreds and thousands. Country hicks and city sophisticates, housewives and whores, drunks and preachers, men and women, young and old; they came because they were lost, and Graham set before them the offer of free salvation.

Night after night, day after day, words came like shots from a siege gun: sin, death, judgment, eternity . . .

"You come. Get up and come right now."

Just as I am, and waiting not,
To rid my soul of one dark blot . . .

And one night a young lad, drawn to the Christ, moved forward with the others. His name was Mike Davis. He wore blue jeans, a knit shirt, and loafers, just like the high school kid that he was. He knew no more of life, the world, death or sorrow than any other kid his age. But he knew the weight of sin and the certainty of his lostness, and he believed there was healing and forgiveness in the Jesus Billy Graham preached.

Meanwhile, under glaring lights on the baseball diamond to the south, I forgot the choir's singing and followed the motion of the pitcher's arm. I stepped toward him as the ball, a blurred, white pellet, came whistling in and broke toward my knees. Whoosh! Crack! I drove it into right center field and dashed toward first base. The runner on second was being waved around third and was digging for home, and on the throw-in I started for second. On the infield grass, the second baseman cut off the throw to home and tried to gun me down at second. I dove head first for the bag, cutting the shortstop's legs out from under him, and we wound up rolling in the dirt, cursing one another. I was safe, and a run was in.

Big deal.

I had no idea that while I swatted at a leather-covered spheroid, my best friend stood on the infield grass of the grandstand to the north, wrestling with eternal issues. I left the ball park that night a lost soul, batting .352 with 20 RBIs. Mike Davis left the fairgrounds batting zero in the world, but saved. A great gulf now separated the two of us. He lived, while I, imagining myself alive, moved among the living dead.

I saw him in church the following Sunday, and he rushed up to me and started talking the strangest stuff.

"I got saved," he said.

And I asked: "You did what?"

"I got saved."

"What's that mean?"

"I went forward in Billy Graham's meetings and received Christ as my Savior. Man, I'm born again!"

I fashioned a lopsided grin and told him that was great, then I quickly changed the subject because I had no idea what he was talking about. He hadn't mentioned religion, nor had he said a word about changing his life. Instead, he trotted out a bunch of mumbo-jumbo about belief in Jesus and receiving Him, and about having a relationship with a man I knew had died centuries ago.

Good grief!

If I said I had a relationship with Lydia E. Pinkham, would that make it true?

4

Well all I want is a party doll,
To come along with me when I'm feeling wild,
To be ever-lovin', true and fair,
To run her fingers through my hair.
~ Buddy Knox ~

Life, life of love poured out, fragrant and holy!
Life, mid rude thorns of earth, stainless and sweet!
Life, whence God's face of love, glorious but lowly,
Shines forth to bow us, Lord, low at thy feet.
~ F. Allenben ~

Do the desires and ambitions of youth seem laughable to you? To me they do not because really they can all be boiled down to certain primary desires and ambitions that one never outgrows. There is a desire to be loved and accepted. There's a desire to be somebody and to do something important. And there's a tremendous desire to feel secure.

And over on the other side, providing the fuel that motivates us to lay hold on these things we imagine will fulfill our deepest desires, are the fears. We look in the mirror at our own pimply faces, and we fear that no one really loves and understands us.

The world is a big, scary place, and we fear we will never find out exactly why we are here, or precisely where we fit in. And above all, we come into the world alone, naked and vulnerable, and this is how we go out. And between cradle and grave we live shut up within ourselves, alone like Coleridge's Ancient Mariner.

But if we can run the fastest, or jump the highest, or roll by in a '55 Chevy, or go steady with the neatest girl or boy, then . . .

Or go to the right schools, or be taken into a good law firm, or buy a house in suburbia, or marry the right person, then . . .

Then we will be fulfilled, and then we will know love and security, and then we will carve an eternal notch in the great gun handle and write our names in the stars.

Except it doesn't work and never will, because death waits to put out the lamp and draw us into the cold and lonely earth, and the living forget us and go about their business. I am filled with a great sadness as I observe the race of man, for no matter who they are or what they are, to me they appear as a pimple-faced man-child in front of a trophy case waiting for someone to come by, stop and say, "You know, I like you." But for many that never happens.

Anyone who entered our high school through the main entrance couldn't help but notice the trophy case, row upon row of golden figures frozen in an eternal moment above words like, *Champions, Midland Conference, 1947*. One day, on a forgotten field of glory, some long-gone hero stripped for the contest, raced toward a distant ribbon, and brought back a glittering piece of metal. *First Place, Summer Games, 1953*.

Such was life in the Republic at mid-century.

All the jocks had a tendency to cluster around the trophy case, as if it belonged to them, which in a sense I suppose it did. This was my place, and I liked it fine.

In the parking lot on the school's south side motorcycles shone beneath the sun. They bore legendary names such as Indian and Harley Davidson. Cars were there too—not your ordinary, run-of-the-mill cars, but souped up machines, lowered, chopped, channeled, with dual carburetors and twin chrome pipes. Long-haired, greasy individuals hung around the machines. They wore black leather jackets and perpetual sneers, and their thoughts ran from sex to booze to fuel injection.

The jocks wore letter jackets and crew cuts, and their thought life occupied a loftier plane than that of the bikers: sex, to football, and back to sex again. No booze or machinery for us, brother! Deep enmity existed between the jocks and the bikers, for no good reason that I can discern. Rather like the world at large, weren't we?

Of course, the girls were there. The bikers had theirs, we had ours.

And wandering around between the two poles represented by jocks and bikers, a group of misfits clung to the strange notion that school actually had something to do with education. They didn't know Willie Mays from Johnny Lujack, but they claimed to have actually read *War and Peace*, to understand that Caesar was Roman, to subscribe to the tenets of Newtonian physics. To some of us, the studiousness of these kids was incomprehensible. They seemed to be throwing their lives away on foolish non-essentials.

But who were Newton and Tolstoy and Tacitus that I should allow them to garbage up my thinking? I had given myself over to the question of whether or not the Elk City defense could stop our single-wing. We were the last major Oklahoma high school football team to operate out of the single-wing, a formation declared obsolete by most authorities, and in a week we were to play our opening game on our field against Elk City. Who knew but that this might be my year to pick up a glittering piece of junk to add to the already cluttered trophy case?

So here we stood one morning, a group of jocks at the trophy case, when, speaking of trophies, down the hall, books in arm, came Connie Mason the cheerleader. She smelled of lilacs—or was it tangerines?—and her eyes were blue as periwinkles. She and two of her friends swayed along, giggling, and looking, but surely not, at me.

"Hi, Doug," she said.

With nothing more than that she threw a switch inside me, and a current surged up from my feet, straight through my head, and up into the stratosphere. Holy Toledo! Did Tacitus know about this?

"You're a devil with the women," said one of my smart-mouthed friends.

Outside, a car rolled by in second, its pipes popping like a machine gun.

"Who is that?" one of the boys asked.

"That's Connie Mason, dummy. Where have you been?"

"Last year she was ugly."

"Last year you were ugly—and dumb."

"She likes you, Miller."

"I don't even know her," I said.

"I'd like to get to know her," said one of our tackles.

"Why, you big, ugly clod," said a skinny halfback, "she wouldn't give you the time of day."

"Is that so?"

"Yeah, that's so."

"Oh, yeah?"

"Yeah!"

The bell silenced this brilliant repartee, and I wandered off to biology to dissect earthworms.

Later that day, on the sidewalk in front of school, I ran into Connie. It was like magic. I was crossing the street from the gym, head down, when I smelled lilacs and tangerines, and there she stood—bobby socks, periwinkle eyes, auburn hair. I stopped as if turned to stone, bereft of the power of speech.

"Are you all right?" she asked.

"Yeah."

"Because you look sick."

"I'm okay. Ah . . . how are you?"

"Fine."

"You're Connie Mason."

"Yes. And you're Doug Miller."

"How do you know?"

"Silly. We were in class together last year. Geometry."

"Oh, sure." *But you weren't this pretty*, I thought.

We got into motion, strolling down the sidewalk, her smiling, me kicking at invisible rocks. I had never felt like such a fool. My tongue wouldn't work. She, on the other hand, seemed perfectly within her element, her element being the boy-girl relationship.

"Are you going to the dance?"

"What dance?"

"The sock hop. After the game next Friday."

In fact, I couldn't dance a lick. "I don't know," I said. "Maybe."

"I hope you'll go," she said. She stopped walking. I stopped. She laid her hand ever so lightly on my arm. "I hope you'll dance with me."

A great knot rose up in my throat and threatened to choke the life out of me. She turned and walked away before I could answer, which was just as well since any answer I might have framed would have been necessarily imbecilic.

We lost the game that Friday, but I got over that minor disappointment in record time, showered, dressed, and rushed to the dance.

The sock hop, a phenomenon of the Fifties, has received a good deal of attention in recent movies. They were called sock hops because the kids took off their shoes and danced in their socks. They danced in their socks because the dances were held in the gyms and the coaches got real hostile about people scarring up the gym floor with street shoes. Back then, white socks were in vogue, for boys and girls. So all these kids would be running around in white socks, dancing a bit, but mostly socializing. We rarely had a live band; instead music came from 45-rpm records spun by a student pressed into the service as an *ad hoc* disk jockey.

I came into the gym from the dressing room. The lights were low, the music moaning. Several couples shuffled around the floor, but most stood in groups laughing and cutting up. I instantly spotted Connie, dancing with a guy who had graduated last year. She spotted me too, but we each pretended not to see the other. She really went into a routine, acting as if she were enjoying herself beyond measure. If she intended to arouse jealousy in me, she succeeded wonderfully, but I maintained my posture and feigned total indifference.

The story of how we circled around one another is long and boring, but I'll cut through the non-essentials and get to the point. Before the evening was over she had maneuvered me into a dark corner of the gym and kissed me full on the lips. And for some time thereafter I was in absolute bondage to her. Her wish became my command.

Connie was an artful conniver, and I a football player of some note. High school girls placed a high premium on football players. I was unattached and available. Connie zeroed in on me. At least that's how it looks to me in retrospect. Connie, if questioned on the subject, might offer a divergent view.

I learned to dance, got a driver's license, gained access to the family car, and whole vistas of living opened before me. It was really great, swaggering down the halls at school with Connie on my arm, stopping to converse with my friends or hers, moving on to loiter outside the classroom until the final bell.

Ah, *Elysium*!

But lightning had killed Rusty Borden, and five missionaries lay in unmarked graves in the jungles of eastern Ecuador, and Billy Graham had come and gone, and I was still unsaved and not sleeping well at night. I had an appointment with God that I had to keep sooner or later, and I was not ready. I, the all-American boy, lived each day in the shadow of death.

5

You guys read too many comic books.
~ James Dean,
in *Rebel Without a Cause* ~

The paths of glory lead but to the grave.
~ Thomas Grey ~

Batter my heart, three-personed God . . .
That I may rise and stand . . . make me new.
~ John Donne ~

I've been confused right from the day I was born.
~ Charley Brown, in *Peanuts* ~

The Fifties kids came of age in cars of various descriptions. In them we learned to make love, make friends, make enemies, dodge the Law. We probably spent more time on wheels than any generation up to that time. They were our homes away from home.

Mike Davis, my best friend, had an old '53 Mercury. In it we cruised up and down Main Street, in and out of drive-ins, along the quiet streets of the suburbs. We saw children in parks, lonely men smoking pipes on porches, heard the raucous din of bars and honky-tonks, saw the rainbow dazzle of neon lights. The car radio wailed: "You don't remember me, but I remember you. 'Twas not so long ago you broke my heart in two. Tears on my pillow. Pain in my heart caused by you—oooo . . ."

"I'm depressed," Davis confessed.

"Me too," I said.

"You? What have you got to be depressed about? You've got it all."

"I've got nothing. Besides, you're the one who has it all. Not long ago you were doing back flips over Jesus. What happened to that?"

"I can't make it work."

"What's to make work?"

"Well, you gotta live it. I can't live it. As long as Billy was here, I was doing great. I went home and told my mom and dad that I was saved. I told all my buddies. They laughed."

"I didn't laugh. I wish I could get saved."

"Why don't you?"

"I don't know how," I said.

"You just have to believe that Jesus died for you . . ."

"Aw look, I know that."

"Do you believe it?"

"I guess so . . . but I ain't saved. I know I'm not. If I was saved I'd know it—wouldn't I? Besides, you're telling me it doesn't work."

"It did for awhile."

"Sure," I said. "For as long as Billy Graham was here."

"Yep. Now I'm back in the same old rut. I wonder how Billy stays at it."

"Preachers are a different breed of cat."

"It don't make sense."

We were quiet for awhile. The radio moaned, "In the still of the night—hite . . . I-yi-yi held you, oh so ti—yite . . ."

Davis said, "I had a little pin, a cross. I pinned it on my shirt and wore it to school. So the boys said, 'What's this, Davis? A new fraternity?' And I said, 'Yeah, it's one that everyone can be in.' And I felt good about standing up for the Lord. Yesterday one of them said something about me being a Bible-thumper, and I called him a sonofabitch and said I was going to knock his teeth out."

I laughed. "I don't think that's the way Jesus did it."

"That's just it," he said. "I don't do anything the way Jesus did it. I can't make it work. I'm worse than ever. I thought when I went forward at Billy's meetings that my whole life was changed. I'm the same old slob I was before."

"Maybe it didn't take."

"Huh?"

"Maybe you didn't get saved."

"But I did. I know I did."

"How do you know?"

"You just know."

"But how do you? Do you hear bells, or see lights, or . . ."

"Aw, shut up!"

"No, I'm not getting cute. I want to know. How do you know if you're saved?"

'You just . . . aw, forget it."

He pulled into the drive at my place and cut the engine, and we sat in utter boredom and depression.

"What happens when you've done it all?" I finally asked.

"Huh?"

"When you've done whatever it is you want to do—then what's left?"

"I guess you roll over and die. What do you want to do?"

"I thought I wanted to play football."

"You're doing it," Davis said.

"Yeah, but . . ."

"And you've got a good-looking girl friend."

"Do you remember when Rusty Borden got killed?"

"Sure."

"I can't forget that," I said. "I keep thinking that he's somewhere right now, alive and conscious. I keep wondering why I'm here and he's there. What if it were me? Man!"

"Yeah," Davis whispered.

I turned to him, the first time I had looked directly at him since we'd pulled into my driveway, and started talking. "Are you afraid to die?" I asked him.

"Yeah," he admitted. "But I know if I do I'll be with the Lord. When I went forward at Billy's meetings, a man gave me a packet of little cards with Bible verses on them. I was supposed to memorize all of them."

"Did you?"

"Naw. I backslid. But I remember one of them. 'To me to live is Christ, and to die is gain.'"

"The Bible says that?"

"Somewhere. I think Paul wrote it."

"To die is gain," I muttered. "I wish I felt that way. All I can think is that I'm standing in front of God, and I feel like I want to hide."

"You need to get saved."

"But how do you do that?"

"You have to believe that . . . Boy, we sound like a broken record."

"Yeah, blah, blah, blah . . ."

Night fell across the city while two kids in a parked car wallowed in depression. One was depressed because he was alive and couldn't seem to show it; the other was depressed because he was dead and didn't know it.

I learned later that at some point during my soul crisis two boys began to pray for me. Neither of them knew of my crisis. In fact, I don't believe I had ever had a conversation with either of them, even to discuss something as mundane as the weather. But for reasons none of us can completely fathom, they started praying for me.

Now most of us assume that being prayed for results in great blessing—which is true. We further assume that blessing makes one feel good and happy—which may be an outright lie. God's blessing may initially drive one further into despair because this is what it may take to get the person being prayed for to cry out for the mercy of God.

So there were these two guys, neither jocks nor bikers, whom I hardly knew. They sat in class with me, rarely said two words, did their work, handed in their assignments, went on their way. But they came together and by mutual agreement entered into an activity that few took note of. Suppose there is a God, and that He is not just some impersonal, amoral force, but an actual person with intelligence and will and emotion. And suppose this God is really aware of what is going on, and that He has plans and purposes that extend to and include people like you and me. And suppose you could talk to this God and ask Him for things and He would answer. What would you ask Him for? Most people wouldn't ask for anything. In fact, most people do not because they don't actually believe any of this. But these two guys, sitting quietly in class day after day, were members of a dwindling minority—born again Christians who believed they could pray and get answers. They began meeting together one evening a week for prayer to this God, about Whom most of us knew precisely nothing. And closeted, they got down on their knees and dealt with eternal issues. While I bent all my efforts to the task of moving an elliptical, leather-covered bladder one hundred yards before the eyes of a thousand screaming aficionados, the two remained at home and talked to God.

The next day my name made the sports page of the newspaper. No one, but no one, paid any attention to the two praying Christians—except for God, and of course God didn't make the sports page either. But somewhere ages and ages hence (if my former English teachers will forgive my shameless plagiarism) the prayers of two quiet kids will bear fruit, and what they were doing was, for me, the most significant thing happening at the time.

But why would they pray for me, whom they hardly knew? Ah, but they knew who I was. What would be the effect on Putnam City High School, they asked one another, if Doug Miller were to get saved? When had one of the hotshot jocks ever gotten saved and then taken a public stand for Christ? It had never happened as far as they could remember. Did they dare to believe that God could reach and save such a person as me? Yes, they did. So they wrote the name Doug Miller on their list, and they took it before their God, who knew all and saw all, and who loved all with undying, unquenchable love, and they prayed, "Father, in the Name of, for the sake of, your Son, our Lord Jesus Christ, we ask you to save Doug Miller."

Their prayers are one of the reasons, I have since decided, that my life began to come unraveled. There was no peace for me. I was like the troubled sea when it cannot rest, whose waters cast up mire and dirt. When a person's sin is upon him, and when he is borne down by the weight of that sin, and possessed of an overwhelming sense of guilt, what does it matter that the world as he knows it is beating a path to his doorstep. The world cannot save him. There is no salvation in the pop of flashbulbs or in a newspaper's print.

6

If you haven't gambled for love in the moonlight,
Then you haven't gambled at all.
~ Frankie Laine ~

All is vanity and vexation of spirit.
~ Ecclesiastes 1:14 ~

Man of Sorrows, what a name
For the Son of God who came
Ruined sinners to reclaim.
Hallelujah, what a Savior!
~Phillip P. Bliss ~

Connie and I were at the lake, having driven there after a football game. Though it was early November, it was unseasonably warm, and the night sky was clear and dusted with stars. Orion wheeled down to the south, the Great Bear stood up in the north, and the rising moon blazed across the water. The wind broke up the lake's surface, and the moon's path became thousands of dancing lights. Then, as the wind died down, the lights merged back to one.

Frankie Laine had a song made to order for this time and place: "Moonlight Gambler." But I wasn't a moonlight gambler. I didn't know who I was or how I fit in. I put the problem to Connie in the form of a question that got right to the point.

"What am I?"

"What?"

"What am I?" I repeated without looking at her, though I heard her shift toward me, and I knew she was staring at me as if I'd gone nuts.

"Doug," she said, "I don't know what you're talking about. I hate it when you're like this."

"I'm talking about life. I'm talking about . . . Connie, I'm talking about why I'm here."

"You know, you're getting impossible. You really are. You haven't said two words all night. What am I? Who am I? I wish I knew what you want. There's not a boy at school who wouldn't trade places with you."

Her voice broke. I turned to her. In the moonlight her face was silver, her eyes teary.

"Connie," I asked, "who was captain of the football team last year?"

"Why?"

"You don't know, do you?"

"I think it was Bill Compton."

"Right. But you had to think about it. What about the year before."

"I have no idea, but . . ."

"It doesn't matter, does it?"

"No it doesn't."

"And you're sitting here with next year's captain, duly elected and sworn."

"I wish I weren't. I'd like to go home."

"Connie, listen to me. I've got problems."

"You? Who would believe it?"

"Yeah, well my whole life consists of a game that doesn't amount to a hill of beans. I'd like to know why God put me here."

"God?" Her voice took on a defensive tone.

"Yes. Do you believe in God?"

"Sure."

"Do you ever pray?"

"Sometimes. I prayed before the cheerleader tryouts."

"But there's got to be more to it than that."

"Why does there? You are so . . . exasperating."

"If there's a God, I want to know what He is and why He put me here. I want to go to heaven when I die. I keep thinking about Rusty Borden."

"That was a year ago. For crying out loud, Doug! Oh, I'm crying. My makeup's ruined. Take me home."

I started the car and drove to the road and out to the highway. Connie and I had nothing to say to one another. She had scooted as far away from me as she could, which didn't matter to me because I was a million miles from her.

Somewhere along the way she said, "Why don't you talk to Jim McIntyre?"

"Jim McIntyre?"

"He seems to know all there is to know about God."

More silence.

"But leave me out of it," she said at length. "I'm not interested in religious problems. I want to go to dances and games and have fun. What's wrong with that?"

"Nothing, Connie. But if there's . . ."

"Yes, if there's a God. If you say that again I'll get out and walk."

Silence again, all the way home.

I had a Saturday morning ritual in those days. It consisted of sleeping until I felt like waking up, then yelling to my kid brother to bring in the morning paper. Then, pillows propped behind my back, I would read about last night's game. On this particular morning there wasn't a great deal to read about, for we had won only by a hair, and my own performance had been something less than stellar. Then I remembered my argument with Connie, and my ability to concentrate on the printed page diminished. I should never have attempted to confide in her. She couldn't keep a secret. Her talents lay in the other area, that of broadcasting information all over the city, and she had probably told all of her friends by now that I had degenerated into some sort of religious freak.

I tossed the paper aside, got up and got dressed. It seemed there was something I was supposed to do, but I couldn't remember what it was. I wandered out to the kitchen, ate a bowl of Wheaties, exchanged monosyllabic pleasantries with the members of my family, who were either in my way or vice versa, and kept wondering what it was I was supposed to do.

The phone rang. It was Connie.

"Look, I'm sorry about what happened last night," she said.

"Yeah, me too."

"I was just down at the drug store. Guess who I saw."

"Either Presley or Gene Vincent."

"Don't be sarcastic. I saw Jim McIntyre."

That was it. That was what I was supposed to do.

"I told him he needed to talk to you."

"You what?"

"Don't yell."

"I don't want to talk to him."

"Last night you seemed bound and determined to know all about God."

"Oh boy! Connie . . ."

"Look, I'm only trying to help. If you think I'm going to spend the rest of my junior and senior years listening to that stuff about the deeper meaning of life . . ."

"Okay. Okay. Thanks."

"Are you coming over later?"

"Yeah."

"Good. But please, no more preaching."

"I'll be my usual carefree self."

"Bye."

"Bye."

"Love you."

I hung up. No need getting passionate with my mother eaves-dropping out in the kitchen.

Now the ball had been put, so to speak, in my court, and the time had come for me to take some action. I did nothing. I had no intention whatever of sitting down in a one-on-one confrontation with Jim McIntyre.

We all knew McIntyre, and we all looked up to him, both figuratively and literally. He had come to our community about a year ago, all six feet eleven inches of him, a sales representative for an outfit that dealt in class rings. A couple of the coaches remembered him when he played basketball at the University of Minnesota, and before long we all understood that a genuine All-American lived and moved amongst us. And almost as quickly we realized that he was not just an ordinary All-American. He came to all the games, got to know the players and coaches. But he talked about Jesus every chance he got.

There was something intimidating about All-American athletes who prayed in public and talked about Jesus. They seemed to know all the right moves and to be one jump ahead of you. If you said Christianity was for old women and weaklings, they simply looked at you, and you found yourself choking on your own words. If you suggested that giving your life to Christ would ruin your future, they said, "Oh, really?" And you were stuck for an answer. They were clean-cut and disciplined, and everything about them said, "Either put up or shut up."

"I don't know who I am."

"No, but I do."

"I don't know where I'm going."

"Do you really want to know?"

"I'm running from God."

"Stop and turn back to face Him."

"But that will cost something."

"Oh, really?"

"You don't understand."

"Oh, really?"

"What's the answer?"

"What the question?"

"How can I know my sins are forgiven?"

"You'll have to come to Christ as Savior and Lord."

"But that will mean changing my whole life."

"It will mean more than that. It will mean death and rebirth. You will yield to Him as absolute Sovereign. No, 'Maybe.' No, 'Sort of.' You come to Him on His terms, not yours. You know what He said to the rich young ruler: 'Either throw it all over and come after Me, or go back to your swimming pool and your vintage wine.'"

I could construct conversations with McIntyre endlessly, and none of them came out the way I liked. So I didn't call him that weekend. I moped about the house feeling sorry for myself, and I hoped my tongue would fall out if I ever again talked to Connie Mason about my soul troubles.

But McIntyre wasn't so easily avoided. Telling him someone was worried about dying and going to hell was like throwing meat to a hungry lion or waving a red flag in front of a bull. The following Monday after football practice I found him waiting for me. The warm weather had gone away overnight, pushed south by a cold front. I left the dressing room with my hands thrust into the pockets of my letter jacket and an American Literature book under my arm.

"Hey, Miller," someone shouted.

It was McIntyre, seated in his car, engine running, heater on, window on the driver's side rolled halfway down. He had on a gray overcoat with the collar turned up, and his gloved hands rested on the steering wheel.

I walked to where he was parked.

"Get in. I'll give you a ride."

Here goes, I thought, as I climbed in on the passenger side. *He'll lay me over the head with Jesus.*

But he did not—not right away at least. Instead he said, "You been sick?"

He backed out of the parking lot and headed east.

"No. Why?"

"You looked sick Friday night against John Marshall."

I laughed. "Thanks," I said. "Any more encouraging words?"

"Yeah," he said. "Play that way against Midwest City and I'll visit you in intensive care."

"Hey, go easy," I told him. "I've been under a lot of pressure."

"I know," he said, and smiled. I immediately knew I had said the wrong thing.

"Aw, you've been talking to Connie Mason. That crazy . . ."

"I thought you liked Connie."

"Yeah, well she can be a real pain in the neck."

"Look, I'm not going to preach to you, because you don't like preachers—right?"

"Right!"

"But you've got problems—right?"

"Maybe," I muttered, looking straight ahead.

"Okay. I want to ask you a question. Don't answer me yet. Just go and think about it. You can tell me later."

"Shoot."

"Who was Jesus?"

"That's the question?"

"That's it."

"Come on. I don't have to think about that. Everyone knows who Jesus was."

"So, who was He?"

"Why, He was a great religious leader. A Jew. But the other Jews didn't believe He was Christ, so they crucified Him."

"And do you believe He was the Christ?"

"Sure. He was the Son of God."

"What's that mean to you?"

I sat. I had no answer. Finally I said, "It means I should try to be like Him."

He nodded. "I'm going to tell you something," he said, "and I want you to think about it." He glanced over at me. "Jesus was God, come to earth as a man."

I turned to stare at him. He was smiling as he drove along.

"Man," I said, "that's crazy."

"Is it? Do you have a Bible at home?"

"Yeah."

"Get it and read the first fourteen verses of *John*. We'll talk about it later."

I lived only a few blocks from school, and it didn't take long to drive. When I jumped out of McIntyre's car in front of my house, I fairly tore across the lawn and bounded through the front door. I threw my lit book on the couch, shucked out of my jacket and headed for my parent's bedroom where the family Bible lay on a lamp table. My mother found me sitting on the edge of the bed, thumbing through the Bible, something that probably took her completely by surprise.

"Supper will be late," she said. "Your dad has to stay late at work."

"Okay," I said. "I'm looking for something here."

"What?"

"*John*. Is there a book called *John*?"

"New Testament," she said.

"Got it," I said. "Here it is."

I read: *In the beginning was the Word, and the Word was with God, and the Word was God. The same was in the beginning with God. All things were made by Him, and without Him was not anything made that was made.*

I read on, verse after verse, to verse fourteen: *And the Word was made flesh and dwelt among us, and we beheld His glory, the glory as of the only begotten of the Father, full of grace and truth.*

"What are you reading?" she asked.

"Listen," I said. I read aloud what I had just read silently. "What does that mean?" I asked.

"I guess," she replied, "that it means what it says."

"But is he saying that Jesus was God?"

"Yes."

"And you believe that?"

"Yes. Don't you?"

I didn't answer. I only sat looking at the words. Never, up to that time, had I been confronted with such an outlandish proposition and then been asked if I believed it. Fact is, I didn't believe it. I had never been asked to believe it, had never been informed that such a belief was necessary. Jesus was a carpenter with a beard, long hair and sandals who walked the dusty roads of Palestine, patted children on the head, told men to love one another. In paintings He herded sheep in green valleys, knocked on doors, hung on a cross. *All things were made by Him, and without Him was not anything made that was made.* The starry universe, the rolling oceans, the whirling, sub-atomic particles . . .

Without Him was not anything made that was made.

I don't recall, over fifty years after the fact, how much time went by before I saw Jim McIntyre again; probably only a few days. But I remember thinking off and on about Jesus, about who He was, and about how absurd it all seemed. I would be walking to school, or sitting in class, or I'd be at home, in my room, bent over a math book, and the thought would come to me afresh: *The Word was made flesh and dwelt among us.* And I would stop in mid-thought, all my attention drawn to John's uncompromising assertion.

The next time I saw McIntyre, he offered to buy me a Coke. He had on the same gray overcoat and the same black gloves. We drove to the drive-in, went inside, sat at a table in the back room.

"Did you read *John*?"

"Yeah." I had been stirring my Coke with the straw. But I stopped and leaned forward, elbows on table. "How could a man be God?"

"Let me ask it another way," he said. "Could God choose to become a man? Does He have the power and the know-how to enter His own creation as a baby and to live out His life and die as a man?"

"I guess so. I guess God could do anything He wanted to. But why would He do it?"

The seconds ticked away.

"To give His life to save guys like you and me."

"To save us from what?"

McIntyre's eyes were gray with flecks of green. I found it hard to look at him directly.

"Are you afraid of death?"

"Ain't everyone?"

"Maybe. Maybe not."

"Look," I said, "if you're so red hot to die, why don't you just go out and jump in front of a Mack truck?"

"I'm not looking for death. The question has to do with fear. Doug, you're afraid to die, aren't you?"

"I keep thinking about Rusty Borden," I told him.

"Why?"

"It could have been me, that's why. One minute you're here, the next you're somewhere else."

"Everlasting life. How does that sound to you?"

"It depends on where you live forever. What if you die and go to hell?"

"Sounds pretty stupid to me. If there's a way to avoid hell, why would anyone be dumb enough to go there?"

"Look, McIntyre, it ain't like I'm trying to go to hell. I just can't seem to do right. I don't understand guys like you and Billy Graham. How do you live a good life?"

"I don't."

"You *don't*?"

"Neither does Graham."

"Aw, man . . ." He was driving me nuts.

"The difference in you and me isn't that you're bad and I'm good," he said. "Christ died to pay the penalty for my sins—for yours too. One day I came to Him and took Him as my Savior. You never have. I'm saved. You—you're as lost as any man ever was. That's why you're afraid to die."

He was right, of course, but he only succeeded in making me angry.

"Listen to me," he said. "I want to give you a Bible verse to think about. 'He hath made Him to be sin for us, who knew no sin, that we might be made the righteousness of God in Him.'"

"I don't understand that."

"It means that He took your sins on Himself, paid for them all, so that you could be credited with His righteousness."

"And my sins . . ."

"Will never be brought up against you."

"How can I know that?"

"God says so. Do you believe it?"

"I don't know."

"Think about it."

"I will."

And off I went, as lost as ever.

7

Wake up, little Susie, wake up!
~ The Everly Brothers ~

I woke, the dungeon flamed with light.
My chains fell off, and I was free.
I rose, went forth, and followed thee.
~ Charles Wesley ~

Thus far did I come loaden with my sin,
Nor could aught ease the grief that I was in . . .
Blessed Cross! Blessed Sepulcher! Blessed rather be
The Man that there was put to shame for me.
~ Christian in *Pilgrim's Progress* ~

Davis, up like a Roman candle, down like the *Titanic*, was up. But I can't get into the full story without laying some groundwork. Allow me, therefore, to digress into an account of Ellie Wassom.

Ellie showed up at church one day as our new youth director, an import from Sioux Falls, South Dakota. Now youth directors, as any fool knows, must be bright, attractive college kids with lots of energy, a stock of funny stories and a copious bag of tricks. The theory is that it takes some clever gimmickry to get kids into church, and that translates into goldfish swallowing, flagpole sitting and so on. Did I hear someone say, "Why not pray for them and give them the Gospel?" My friend, you are hopelessly bogged down in 19th Century thinking. But, then, so was Ellie.

She weighed over two hundred pounds, wore dresses and shoes that went out of style in the Twenties, and had thick, rimless glasses.

But her real secret popped out the minute she opened her mouth—she was another Jim McIntyre. I had begun to notice a curious familial resemblance between all these fanatics. They didn't talk religion, they talked Jesus. If you said, "Look, my life's messed up," they talked Jesus. "You don't understand, I'm afraid of death." More Jesus. No matter how complicated or complex the problem, their solution had something to do with Jesus.

Our former youth director had been a cheerleader at a local university. She was bright, witty, attractive, offensive to none. Everyone had fun. No one got upset.

And no one got saved.

Then, down from the plains of Dakota came Ellie Wassom, neither witty nor attractive, who had apparently been matriculated in the same school as Jim McIntyre, and everyone's life started getting rearranged—beginning with Mike Davis.

I probably should explain that Mike and I did not go to school together; we knew each other from church. I went to a school in the suburbs while he went to an inner-city school directly across the street from the church we had both attended for years. It was easy for Mike, when he left school, to go by the church to see Ellie, which is exactly what he began doing. For Mike (though I didn't recognize it at the time) was another Jim McIntyre. Immature and shaky, yes, but born again and bearing the image of the Christ and the soul of the true believer; thus, he was drawn to Ellie, a woman with whom he seemed to have nothing in common, and they came together like the Bobbsey twins at Clover Bank.

"Mike," Ellie would say, "you're living on raw emotion and nothing more. Do you think God has changed, or His Word has changed, just because you got up this morning feeling rotten?"

And Mike, bewildered, would raise his eyebrows and shrug his shoulders.

"Mike," she would ask, "how often do you pray? And how much? And what do you pray about? You know, this bless mommy and daddy stuff won't get it."

And Mike would scratch his head.

"The Book, Mike. The Book. The Book. What did you get out of God's word today?"

"Well, ah . . ."

"You got nothing."

"Well, ah . . ."

"Because you didn't open it."

"I didn't have time."

"You'll have to take time—or flounder along from one disaster to another."

Hard words, but true.

"Mike, let's pray. Let's pray together. This youth group is as sorry looking an outfit as I've ever seen. How many do you think are actually saved?"

"I don't think any of them are."

"Neither do I. Glad we agree. Which ones, if they did get saved, would influence the others?"

"Well, Nancy McNatt. She's sort of the leader of the group. And Doug Miller."

"I know about him. He plays football."

"Yeah."

"I see him in church on Sunday mornings, but he never comes out to the youth meetings."

"Why should he? It's boring. But I'll tell you something about him. He told me once that he wished he was saved but he didn't know how to be."

"He said that?"

"Yes."

"Great Scott! Write his name down and let's pray for him."

One of the first things Ellie did was get the youth meeting out of the church building; she said she didn't like the ecclesiastical atmosphere; she believed that religiosity stifled the sort of spontaneity and freedom of expression she was after. When a kid came into church he switched gears, put on his religion mask. Ellie wanted to get the kids to sit down together in their own milieu, and there she wanted to present them with the claims of Jesus Christ and force them to the consideration that He is a real, living Savior who demanded control of their entire existence. In the bedroom, the classroom, the kitchen, the den, on the street corner, in the parking lot—He insisted on nothing short of total sovereignty.

So on a Sunday afternoon in early February of 1957, a handful of kids got together in the home of Nancy McNatt. The handful amounted to six, to be more specific. Nancy was there, and Mike Davis, Nancy's friend Angie, a boy named Billy Reynolds, who seemed the very epitome of teenage confusion, another named Rob Horner, possessed of a baby face and an emotional immaturity to match it, and a pugnacious kid named Patricia Margaret but who called herself Pattie. She had the uncanny ability to turn neutral discussions into full-scale brawls.

In any group, one individual usually emerges as the stabilizer. Nancy assumed this position. Rob never seemed to know exactly why he was there. Davis was the court jester. Billy Reynolds wore a brown leather jacket summer or winter, greased his hair, chewed gum, got on Pattie's nerves. He believed no one understood him. Pattie believed she could read him like a book and knew him for the obnoxious whiner he was. A more unlikely bunch could scarcely be imagined. Only Nancy could have actually been called religious, which just meant she had learned to fake it better than the others. Yet God, as it turned out, had chosen these kids as His unwitting instruments. Through them He would shake Oklahoma City teenagers to their crazy foundation whether they liked it or not. Spiritual reality was about to greet them in the person of Jesus Christ, the Son of the Living God.

Ellie got the meeting going with a prayer, then Nancy passed around oatmeal cookies and strawberry Kool-Aid.

Time came for the usual canned devotional, delivered by Mike. He had this booklet from a place in Nashville that was supposed to contain nice thoughts to warm the juvenile heart. He sat cross-legged on the floor, as did the others, except for Ellie who, if she got down there, couldn't have gotten back up. She sank down on the couch. Davis held the booklet up between thumb and forefinger as if it were contaminated.

"This thing stinks," he said.

Nancy raised her eyebrows. Angie giggled. Ellie sat on the couch like the Buddha at Kamakura. Billy chewed his gum, profoundly bored. Rob took up space. Pattie flew to the attack.

"I suppose you can write a better one."

"Yeah," Davis modestly admitted, "I can write a better one."

"Well, why don't you, Hemingway?" Pattie asked.

"Did you ever wonder what hell is like, Pattie?" Davis asked.

"Aw, come on," said Billy Reynolds. "How dumb can you get?"

"I read this sorry book," said Davis. "It says nothing about sin, nothing about hell, nothing about salvation."

Ellie interrupted. "Did any of you ever hear Jesus called the Savior?"

"Yes," Nancy said.

"Who did He save?"

"Why . . . us."

"What did He save us from?" Ellie asked.

Nancy swallowed. No one said a word.

"If He's the Savior, He has to save someone from something," Mike said, and threw the booklet on the floor in the middle of the circle. "If not, then He's not a savior at all. Whoever heard of a savior who didn't save somebody from something?"

"This is dopey," Pattie said.

"Goofy," said Billy Reynolds.

"Okay, Billy," Mike said. "If it's goofy, then explain it."

"Nuts," said Billy.

"Look," Mike said, "we all know each other. We all go to school together. Are we Christians?"

A few heads nodded tentatively.

"Then how are we any different from the other kids who don't go to church and who don't even claim to be Christians?"

"We're here, aren't we?" Pattie insisted.

"Yeah," said Rob, as if to convince himself he was part of the gathering. His baby face flushed slightly, and sweat showed a bit over his upper lip.

"Oh, we're here all right," Mike answered. "But Ellie asked a simple question and no one can answer it. What did the Savior save us from?"

"From our sins," Nancy blurted.

"Okay," Ellie said. "But why? What's so bad about sin that it took the death of God's Son to save us?"

No one said a word.

Finally Mike Davis took it up: "And how did we get saved? I was reading the other day where Jesus said He came to seek and save the lost. Are we lost?"

"Not me," said Pattie. "I've been in church all my life. I joined the church and was baptized when I was ten years old."

Suddenly gum-chewing Billy Reynolds dropped the bomb: "I think I'm lost."

"Billy . . ." Nancy began.

"I'm not lost," Pattie declared.

"Wait," Ellie Wassom said. The couch groaned as she leaned forward. "Why do you think you're lost, Billy?"

"I must be," he said. "I don't understand what you and Davis are talking about."

Ellie said, "I've known lots of lost people who didn't know they were lost. But I've never known a saved one who didn't know he was saved. Where does that leave you, Billy?"

He bit his lower lip and frowned. "I guess I'm lost."

"You are not!" Pattie said.

Ignoring Pattie, Ellie said, "There's a verse in the Bible that says the Spirit bears witness with our spirit that we are children of God."

"I don't get it," Rob said.

"That means," said Ellie, "that saved people know if they are saved because the Holy Spirit tells them so."

"The Holy Spirit ain't told me nothing," said Billy.

"Me neither," Rob said.

"I'm not lost," Pattie said.

"Then Jesus must not have died for you," said Mike Davis.

"He did too," Pattie said.

"If you're not lost and never were then He didn't come for you because He said He came to seek and save the lost."

"Listen, buster . . ."

"All right, let's calm down," Ellie said. "Mike, why don't you tell us how you got saved?"

Mike nodded. "Sure," he said. "You gotta remember, I grew up in church. I went every Sunday. I got baptized when I was ten years old, just like Pattie. But I didn't get saved. I was no more a Christian than a baboon. Then Billy Graham came to town, and my mom dragged me out to see him. That first night I saw people going forward to accept Christ that I'd known all my life. I saw them in church every

Sunday. I couldn't understand why they were going up there. They were already Christians—I thought. Boy, that shook me up.

"I didn't want to go back, but my mom dragged me out there again. Billy was talking about the rich, young ruler, how he came to Jesus looking for eternal life but went away when he thought the price was too steep. I got wondering what I would have to give up to follow Jesus. And before long Billy started talking about repentance, and I knew I'd have to lose my whole life. I didn't want to do that because I liked things like they were—I thought.

"I was sort of like Billy Reynolds. The longer I listened to Billy, the more I realized I was lost. I had never been saved. This meeting with Christ he kept talking about was something I'd never had. I was in my sin, and I knew it.

"One night he quoted John 3:16. I had heard it all my life, but I never had really *heard* it. 'For God so loved the world that He gave His only begotten Son, that whosoever believeth in Him should not perish, but have everlasting life.' It was like a light came on in my head. I almost ran forward that night when he gave the invitation. The funny thing is that I knew, absolutely knew from that moment, that I was saved and that I would never be the same."

He stopped talking. No one spoke. Nancy started to cry. Billy Reynolds looked like he'd been pole-axed.

"Let's pray," Ellie said. "Mike, why don't you lead us in prayer?"

It was the first time Mike had prayed in public. He was far from eloquent, but that probably didn't matter.

Our church was like many others. Born years before in the white heat of revivalism, off and running with a divine energy that carried it all over the globe, it had succumbed in the 19th Century to higher criticism and a gospel of good works mixed with an American rendition of social Darwinism, had slowed to a crawl, and had solidified into an institution. Most of its preachers came from a Dallas seminary that specialized in blasphemy. In their homiletics courses they taught the fledgling seminarians how to prepare neat, canned, professional sermons and how to deliver them in an acceptable fashion. They taught them how to marry and bury, how to intone the rituals in baptism and communion with proper solemnity. Then they taught them just enough Greek and Hebrew to be dangerous, and sent them out into the world ignorant, in many cases, of God's salvation and the grace of the Lord Jesus Christ.

But God was weaving His tapestry, in spite of all this, and He weaves a wonderful work. Its separate strands seem confusing and unrelated, but it all comes together in a miraculous pattern, and only afterwards can we discern what it's all about. Five missionaries are killed in Ecuador. Rusty Borden is hit by lightning. I come under heavy conviction about my sin and my unsaved soul. Billy Graham comes to town. Mike Davis gets saved. Two non-descripts begin praying for me. Jim McIntyre tells me Jesus is God. Ellie Wassom shows up. Davis gets his feet under him, preaches to the kids at the youth meeting, shakes them up something awful.

Out of habit, and nothing more, I showed up at church Sunday morning, a week after Davis wrought havoc in the youth meeting, and I heard a statement from the pulpit that lodged in my brain like a dart. The preacher, who could not preach, up before a congregation that did not care to listen, thrust his fist toward the ceiling and cried, "There is a fountain filled with blood, drawn from Immanuel's veins, and sinners plunged beneath that flood lose all their guilty stains."

He was a terrible excuse for a preacher. Why should he, of all people, have been able to say something that created in me a curious ache? If only I could get to that fountain. That must have been why I went out to the church meeting that evening. I must have been looking for that fountain.

Not many showed up for Sunday evening services. There were two old women, retired school teachers, who always sat in the same spot, up front and over to the right. And also always at their favored spot (up front and over to the left) were an old couple who never missed a service so far as I know. I was never sure what he got out of being there, for he always seemed to be asleep. Another perennial was a woman who worked as a reporter for a local newspaper. A choir occupied the choir loft, but it wasn't the choir that sang on Sunday mornings, although the choir director and the organist were the same. The Sunday evening choir was composed of individuals drafted into duty on an *ad hoc* basis. They were there, and someone laid hold on them. It was a nice thing if they could carry a tune but not an actual requirement.

Ellie Wassom led in the youth group. They had met at about five-thirty at Rob Horner's house; church started at seven. It was the usual group, the kids I went to Sunday school with in the morning: Nancy McNatt, Angie, Pattie, Rob Horner, Billy Reynolds, Mike. They clustered together in the back of the sanctuary, staring vacantly about, whispering, and giggling. Mike Davis detached himself from them and came up to sit with me, about half-way back in the middle section.

In those days the service followed a prescribed order. There would be a song or two by the congregation, a prayer by the preacher, a song by the makeshift choir. Then the preacher would give a message, and there would be an altar call. This altar call should not be confused with the altar calls of Charles Finney and D.L. Moody, in which sinners came to be saved. Rather, it was just a time for any who wished to come and kneel at the altar and pray. The lights would be dimmed, the organ playing softly, and the mood would be very solemn and churchy.

On this particular evening, however, things went completely haywire. The songs were sung, the prayer prayed, the sermon (such as it was) preached; but the altar call got out of hand.

"Now any who wish may come and spend some time quietly with the Lord," said the preacher.

"Hold on there," someone said.

Everything stopped, and all eyes went toward the voice, and toward a gum-chewing, pimple-faced kid in a leather jacket who moved down the aisle to the altar.

"What's he up to?" I asked Davis.

He shrugged and shook his head.

At the front of the room, beneath the pulpit where the poor, confused preacher stood, Billy Reynolds stopped and turned back to face the equally confused worshipers.

"I'm saved," he said, just like that. "I'm saved," he repeated, "and I know it. God so loved the world that He gave His Son to die for me. I was lost, but now I'm saved. Jesus saved me."

And he walked back and sat down.

"Holy mackerel," I whispered.

Suddenly someone stirred off on the periphery. The old man who always seemed asleep came slowly to where Billy Reynolds had been.

Having arrived out of breath, he waited for a moment. Finally he said, "It's been years since I have heard words such as saved and lost. I, too, was saved when I was about that young man's age. I was saved in a meeting where Billy Sunday was preaching. That man talked about sin and hell, and I knew I had to get saved. It's a wonderful thing to be saved, a wonderful thing . . ."

And the strangest thing happened. The old man began to cry like a baby and had to be helped back to his seat.

People sat rooted like trees. The preacher was like the proverbial fellow who went out hunting a rabbit and jumped up a bear. He didn't know what to do.

Someone else stood up to testify. Then Mike Davis gave his testimony.

By now I don't believe there was a dry eye in the house. But for me that part was, and is, of no consequence. The scales fell from my eyes. I believed that Jesus was both Lord and Christ, and that He died for me. I trusted Him, and in that moment I was born again.

8

Salvation, salvation, vast, full and free;
Thro' the precious blood of the Son of God
Who was slain on Calvary.
~ T.D.W. Muir ~

Is it bigger than a bread box?
~ Steve Allen ~

Many people, all unsaved, have asked me what I mean when I talk of salvation and rebirth. Is it an experience? Yes, it is an experience, as concrete and real as anything a human may undergo. But how do you know when, or if, it has taken place? These subjective religious events, which can't be documented, verified, measured or otherwise delineated and analyzed, are always looked upon with extreme skepticism, particularly by the so-called intelligentsia. There is nothing wrong, in my opinion, with honest inquiry, and Christians should be ready to defend their faith, on intellectual grounds or any other.

All religions have their adherents who claim to have had mystical encounters with deity, and all claim to have had divine revelations of one sort or another. The Muslim cry, "There is no God but Allah, and Mohammed is His prophet," is no less compromising than the Christian claim that salvation is through Christ and through Him alone. Which is right?

I cannot go into a protracted apologetic for Christianity at this time. There will be another time and place for that. I will say only that the Bible is a true account. I was saved because by an act of His divine will God, who is sovereign, revealed His Son as Savior to me. The Holy Spirit's part in all this is absolutely essential. He moves to awaken us, to assure us that we are in fact saved, and He begins to work in us to conform us to the image of Christ. This is as close as I can come to explaining what it is to be saved and reborn. Though the intellect plays a part, the process is not entirely intellectual. Some of the most intelligent people I have ever known have been Christians; some have been atheists. Though the emotions may come into play, it is not necessarily an emotional thing. Some people cry when they are saved; others, such as myself, go through the experience dry-eyed. Some can pinpoint, in time and space, the exact moment of conversion; others cannot. But all saved men and women have come to a point of recognizing God's Word as true and by faith have acted on that Word.

All true faith is expressed in action. Suppose, for example, I enter a room occupied by several people, and I announce I've just heard that within five minutes a meteor will fall on that room and pulverize it. Have I told the truth? The real test of whether the people in room believe me is not that they sit there saying they believe me, but what actions they take to avoid the impending disaster. They may begin discussions about my character and whether I typically tell the truth. They may talk of recent weather reports, sunspots, the movement and velocity of meteors. But one thing is certain—those who believe me will get up and leave the room. Those who don't probably won't act at all, though they may continue to talk a good deal. Two men, both thieves, were crucified on either side of Jesus. One railed on Him. The other acknowledged Him as Lord, asked to be remembered when He came into His Kingdom, and was in Paradise with Him that very day. I don't understand why one believed and the other was hostile. Two men may stand side by side while the Bible is read publicly. One hears the Word of God, the other hears only words. I don't pretend to know why.

Salvation takes place when an individual who has been spiritually blind suddenly has his eyes opened so that he perceives as never before the absolute truth of Scripture. Jesus is exactly who He claimed to be and did exactly what He said He'd come to do. And this involves me, personally and directly.

Of course, I found myself thinking, after I was saved, it is so simple and clear that a three-year-old child could see it. I have spent much of my life since then wondering why the bulk of humanity cannot.

9

I refuse to answer on the grounds that it may tend
To incriminate me.
~ Someone before the House
Un-American Activities Committee ~

The next night back at Metre he did not tell the girl
he went upstairs with at the Villa Rossa about Jesus.
And he never told anybody.
~ Ernest Hemingway, *In Our Time* ~

Ask ye what great thing I know,
That delights and moves me so?
What the high reward I win?
Whose the Name I glory in?
Jesus Christ, the crucified.
~ Johann C. Schwedler ~

Monday morning dawned, and I jumped out of bed, same legs, arms, eyes and ears I possessed when I had risen the morning before. But in another way it was a different me, and I knew it. The very atmosphere seemed somehow lighter and purer.

Question: What do I do now?

Fact is, I didn't know, but I felt like I should do something.

I returned that day to the halls of Putnam City High School and plunged back into a lifestyle that had altered not one whit and was not about to do anything to accommodate me in my new faith. The same guys told the same jokes in front of the trophy case near the school's entrance. The same girls swayed by in the same old way, evoking the same passions and lusts in me. The same motorcycle gang parked in its appointed spot in the school parking lot. The same music issued from car radios. Elvis Presley declared that someone he knew wasn't nothin' but a houn'dawg.

The night before, on my way home from church, I had been determined to tell someone at school that I had been saved. Now here I was, and there they were, but I told none of them. I had something they needed. At the very least I ought to fly my colors, let them know where I stood. But how should I begin? Should I just walk up and start in? Should I confront an entire group? Or should I get them one by one? Then I found myself wondering what I was so afraid of. The answer was clear. I did not feel physically threatened, but I was frightened to death of social ostracism, of being laughed at because of being un-cool. I believe I could have handled physical violence, but the idea of the entire school snickering and whispering behind my back was more than I could take. So I went about business as usual, not sure what to do about Jesus or how to do it—not sure, moreover, that I would do anything.

Connie Mason and I met at some point, just as we always did. She began talking about things she considered important, the way she always did. But for some reason, she didn't reach me. It was as if she stood on the other side of some invisible barrier, and her words were garbled in transmission. It occurred to me that she and I had nothing whatever in common. In fact, it occurred to me that I had nothing in common with any of those who only yesterday had been my closest friends. I began to be overwhelmed by a sense of loneliness.

"Are you listening to me?" I heard Connie saying.

"Sure," I heard myself reply.

"Well, are you going or not?"

"Going to what?"

"You didn't hear a word I said."

"I'm sorry," I said. "I just . . ."

"Oooo . . ." she uttered, stamping her foot, and whirling about, she bolted down the hall.

I guessed she would recover from whatever ailed her. I had more pressing problems. I was, let's face it, a pure and simple coward afraid to publicly admit my connection with a man who had died for me. Maybe I could run after Connie, catch her, look her in the eye, say,

"Look at me. I'm saved." But she had already made it clear that she wanted no part of God, or religion, or soul problems.

I wished Jim McIntyre or Ellie were around. Or I wished Mike Davis went to my school so that I had some other Christian to talk to. In fact, I didn't know one person in the whole school who was saved and who would understand anything about the Christian life.

Wait a minute! Come to think of it, I did too. Well, I didn't actually know him, but I knew of his existence because of a speech he had given one day.

I was taking this class called Elements of Public Speaking (or some such thing) as an elective in lieu of Algebra II. I had begun the year in algebra, but I had quickly decided that it required more effort that I wished to expend, so I had rushed down to the office, dropped algebra and switched over to speech.

The teacher, Mrs. Wood, was young and attractive and notably biased toward athletes. She was also plagued with a host of bums like me who had washed up in her class because they were looking for a snap course. We would muster in at fourth hour and wear one another out with speeches that would put an insomniac to sleep. Poor Mrs. Wood, so dedicated, so serious about her calling, only to be hamstrung by a collection of buffoons and cut-ups.

But some of the students in her class seemed actually to be trying to learn how to speak effectively, and one of these was Bill Sam Knight. He had a great deal of difficulty speaking in front of people, for he was shy and quiet and had a slight speech impediment. I, on the other hand, could babble on endlessly on just about any subject under the sun—and would at the drop of a hat. Babbling, of course, was about the extent of my contribution.

One of our assignments earlier in the year had been to sell something. It could be anything we wanted, but we had ten minutes to get up there and convince the class that whatever we were selling was something they couldn't do without. I've long since forgotten what I attempted to sell, but I'll never forget Bill Sam's speech. Amid the pitches for soap, cosmetics, chewing gum, and bicycles, he jumped up there and went into a spiel about the Gospel. At the time, I had been both amazed and mortified—amazed that anyone would do what he had done, mortified on his behalf because he didn't have sense enough to realize that he had made a public spectacle of himself.

Now, many months later, isolated from the student body in my new-found faith, I sought out Bill Sam, the only person I knew who had grit enough to admit to a connection with Jesus Christ. As fourth hour got under way, I slid my chair over toward his. He probably had no idea what I was up to, because prior to this he and I hadn't exchanged more than a half-dozen words.

"Hey," I whispered.

"How ya doing?" he asked.

"Great. Yeah, just great. Listen, I got saved . . ."

"Oh? When . . ?"

"Last night."

I don't know what reaction I expected. If shouts and double-back flips, I was in for a disappointment. He simply sat there, pursed his lips, nodded and said, "I've been praying for you."

I was stunned. "You have?"

He nodded again. "Yep." He didn't seem the least bit surprised. "Me and Joe Hanks."

"Hanks?"

"You know him?"

"Yeah."

"We've been praying for you."

"Why?"

"We figured you needed to get saved."

"How did you know I wasn't?"

He smiled and shook his head. I could hardly have asked a more stupid question. No one in his right mind could have mistaken me for a Christian.

"I'm saved," I said, somewhat dumbfounded by the fact.

About that time Mrs. Wood came in and got the class under way.

"Talk to you later," he said.

Later was after class. We walked down the hall together, I toward a fifth hour study hall, he toward some other class.

"How long have you been saved?" I asked.

"Six years."

We walked on in silence, bumping into scrambling, shouting students.

"Look," I finally said, "I don't know what to do."

"Who said you're supposed to do something?"

"Well—ain't I?"

"Enjoy yourself," he said. "You've got all eternity. Think of it. You're on your way home. Enjoy the Lord. Did He tell you to do anything?"

"I just figured . . ."

"When it's time for you to do something, He'll let you know."

Then we ran smack into Connie Mason, dashing along who-knew-where.

"There you are," she said.

"In person," I replied.

"See you later," said Bill Sam.

"Okay. When?"

"Pretty soon."

"Who's that?" Connie wanted to know, gesturing toward Bill Sam after he was out of earshot.

"Bill Sam Knight," I told her. "He's my friend."

"Him?"

"Yeah. He's a Christian."

Her smirk said, "Uh-oh, here we go again." But when she spoke, she said, "Are we going to the dance?"

"What dance?"

"I knew it. You never listen to me. I told you this morning. The dance at the American Legion Hall. Friday night."

"I don't know," I said.

"You don't know? Well, this is just super!"

"Connie, I . . . I got saved."

There. Now it was said. It hadn't been so difficult after all. But Connie was having all sorts of difficulties with it. She regarded me as if I had metamorphosed into some species of insect. Franz Kafka should have been there to record the event for posterity. Connie, desiring the things most high school girls desire, had made the obvious move and laid hold on the captain of the football team, only to find him a moonstruck fool. Now she was stuck. Or was she?

Genuinely hurt and confused, she wandered away. I had an urge to run after her, thought better of it, and instead went to study hall.

Basketball season was well under way. After school I went to practice. I hadn't lost any ability so far as I could tell, but I was keenly aware of the new relationship that existed between me and the other players. It seemed I had little to say to them, but for some reason I didn't care. As Bill Sam had said, I was on my way home.

That night I got two phone calls. The first was from Jim McIntyre, and he wasted no time in coming right to the point.

"Miller, this is McIntyre. Are you still afraid to die?"

I had to think a moment, because that part hadn't actually occurred to me. "No," I said. I began to laugh. "No, that's gone."

"How does freedom feel?"

"Great. I feel like a load's fallen off."

"Just remember—and never forget it—your freedom cost God the death of His Son."

"I know."

"Start reading *Romans*. New Testament. I'll be in touch."

"Hey, how did you know I got saved?"

"It's all over school."

"I only told two people."

"Well one of them must work for NBC News."

"Connie Mason," I said.

"Okay. The word's out. Now you'll have to live it. Either that or put your Lord to an open shame."

"How do I live it? What do I do?"

"Pray—and read *Romans*."

After I had hung up, I began to be afraid. I mulled over what McIntyre had said about shaming the Lord, and I became convinced that this was exactly what I would do. "No, Lord," I found myself saying. "I can't. I just can't."

The phone rang again. This time it was Connie.

"I'd like to know what's going on," she said.

"I got saved," I said. "What more can I tell you?"

A long silence followed.

"But what are you going to do?" she finally asked. She sounded a lot like me.

"What do you expect me to do?"

"How should I know? But if you're going to be like Jim McIntyre . . ."

"An All-American. I'll settle for that."

"Or that guy you were with today."

"Bill Sam. What's wrong with him?"

"He's weird."

"Maybe everyone else is weird. Maybe he's how people ought to be."

"Oh, so I guess I'm weird."

"Look, all I know is that I'm saved and I'm different. Nothing's the same."

She sighed.

"What about the dance?" I asked.

"Can you still go to dances?"

"I guess so."

"I thought that religious folks didn't dance, smoke, or chew—or go with girls who do."

"No one told me that."

"I can't get another date now."

"Guess you're stuck with me then."

"But if you start preaching, I'll leave."

"Good grief, Connie, what do you take me for?"

She didn't say, but it couldn't have been anything very good.

10

Take my hand, I'm a stranger in paradise . . .
~ from *Kismet* ~

"I am the Lord of the dance," said He.
~ Sydney Carter ~

The years have rolled away, and the past is awash in the sort of misty gold of which legends are spun. Kim Novak dances on the dock in a Kansas town while Mancini plays "Moonglow." Marlon Brando puts on a black leather jacket, kicks a motorcycle into roaring life, becomes the "Wild One." James Dean, beautiful child of a long, lost summer, finds no cause worthy of rebellion. Bogart ("Here's looking at you, kid . . .") succumbs to cancer, leaves Lauren Bacall to wander alone on the beach of Key Largo. Robert Stack drinks himself into oblivion in "Written on the Wind." Ike, whom everyone likes, puts a staggering $71,000,000,000 budget before Congress (Pardon me while I remove my tongue from my cheek). The Coasters are searching every whi-i-ich a-way for Youngblood, about whom the Diamonds also wail, but they call her Little Darlin' (*boom, boom, boom-di-wadah*).

The Fifties rock on toward their bitter-sweet finale, but I am unable to follow them, having heard the music of a different Drummer. I tried, I really tried, but I could not keep a foot in both camps at the same time.

The night was cold and clear, the wind moaning in the bare branches of great elms; and the stars were cold too, high up in the blackness of heaven.

What is man that Thou art mindful of him?

But the American Legion Hall had been lit up like a pinball machine, and shafts of light issued from its windows in bars across the dead lawn. The twang of electric guitars rippled out for blocks all around. I could hear the singer from the parking lot:

> "I know a cat named Way-Out Willie.
> "He got a cool little chick named Rockin' Billie.
> "They walk and stroll and Suzie-Q,
> "And do that crazy hand jive too . . ."

The parking lot was jammed with cars—Dave Winchell's Chevy with the pin-striping, Herbie Turner's Ford with chrome pipes, Chuck Johnson's old Packard that sometimes ran and sometimes didn't. Nashes and Model-A's and Pontiacs were there, and pickup trucks of various types and sizes.

Connie and I pulled up in my dad's Plymouth, parked, and headed for the front door to get out of the bitter cold. I don't know if it is still in vogue, but in those days girls who went with athletes usually wore their letter jackets. Connie had my jacket. I had on a leather jacket and gloves.

We opened the door. The music struck like a trip-hammer:

> "Doctor and lawyer and Indian chief,
> "They all dig that crazy beat.
> "Way-Out Willie gave 'em all a treat,
> "When he did the hand jive with his feet . . ."

"Hey, Miller, come on in," someone shouted. It was Joe Ed Tracy, our fullback.

"Joe Ed," I shouted back. "What's shaking?"

"Everything," he shouted.

He was on the dance floor with Abby French, doing a dance called the Bop, which has long since gone the way of all flesh. There must have been a hundred people jammed onto that floor, wiggling and shaking.

Connie and I joined them, coats and all. The heat of the moment was astounding. The song ended, then another began, and another. The band seemed set to play for a non-stop record. The windows and light fixtures vibrated. Sound penetrated the roof, rebounded off the far galaxies. Youth, everlasting youth, pulsated in a ritual as old as the race. It was the mating dance, the war dance, the rite of passage, the baptism of fire, the gentile bar mitzvah, the initiation into mysteries.

The music slowed. The lights dimmed. *Earth angel, earth angel, will you be mine?* Dancer clung to dancer, oozed about the floor, a part of a great wheeling mass, and returned to the point of departure.

The music stopped. We moved to the tables along the wall, removed our coats and heaped them up together.

"I hear strange things about you, son," Joe Ed Tracy said.

Connie went rigid, and so did I. I fashioned a grin, chuckled, and asked what he was talking about.

"I hear you went religious on us."

Abby French was there, and Lou Ann Sanders, Dave Winchell, Chuck Johnson, and Charlene Hardison.

I knew right then that silence or outright denial would never work, except at the price paid long ago, with bitter tears, by the fisherman called Simon Peter. To be one of the boys again, I would have to say publicly, "I never knew Him."

Joe Ed grinned; the others waited.

"What's so crazy about religion?" I asked.

"I don't know," he replied. "Don't know a damned thing about it."

"Doug's on his way to Africa to convert the Watutsis," Connie said.

I could have strangled her, but I restrained myself.

"Well, come on," said Joe Ed, and clapped me on the back. "Tell me about salvation."

"Jesus died for me," I said. "You too, buddy."

"And that's it?"

"Ain't that enough?"

"I don't get it," said Lou Ann Sanders.

"Doctor Livingston, I presume," said smart-mouthed Connie.

"Aw, shut up, Connie," I said.

"Don't tell me to shut up!"

"I joined the church myself when I was in junior high," said Chuck Johnson.

"That's not what Doug is talking about," Abby French said, staring at me.

"Well," Chuck said, "the way I look at it one religion is as good as another, as long as you're sincere."

"That isn't what he's talking about," Abby insisted. She sounded almost angry.

"Well what in hell is he talking about?" Joe Ed wanted to know.

No one was grinning by now, and no one was laughing.

"Remember when Rusty Borden got killed?" I asked Joe Ed.

He shrugged and looked at his feet.

"I couldn't sleep for a long time," I said. "I kept trying to figure out what it would be like to suddenly be dead."

"Wouldn't be like nothing," Dave Winchell said. "Dead is dead."

"I don't believe it," I answered, still looking directly at Joe Ed, who still stared at his feet. "I believe Rusty is wide awake somewhere, right now. I believe if you could talk to him right now he'd tell you that if you miss Jesus you've missed it all."

"Miss all of what?" Lou Ann Sanders asked.

"Life, the whole point of life. What does anything else matter if in the end you die and go to hell?"

"My preacher doesn't believe in hell," said Lou Ann.

"We're all going to die," I said. "I know that Jesus can give us eternal life. You say that's crazy. I say it's all that really matters."

"How do you know that?" Joe Ed demanded, and turned his eyes up from the floor to glare at me.

"I read it in the Bible," I said.

"And you believe that?"

"I believe that."

"Well I'll be damned."

"Look," I said, "you'd just as well get used to the idea. The old Doug Miller is gone. The rest of you can do what you want. I'm going with the Lord. He died to save me."

"From what?" someone asked.

"From sin," I answered.

The music started, and couples began to drift away. Connie, enraged and helpless, had disappeared (to the ladies' room, I later learned), and only Joe Ed and Abby French remained.

"What in the hell is the matter with you, boy," Joe Ed asked.

"I'm saved," I said. "I don't know how else to tell you."

"Well, a good man bites the dust. Come on, Abby, let's dance. I sure as hell ain't saved."

But Abby was still staring at me. "They're the ones who are all wrong," she said. "I don't think you're crazy at all. I think . . . I think . . ." And tears spilled out of her dark eyes and rolled down her cheeks. She dashed away. Joe Ed looked to her, back to me, and with a growl went after her. I was left alone, on the edge of the dance floor, while guitars twanged and the singer moaned:

"Gather round me, buddies,
"Hold your glasses high,
"And drink to a fool, a crazy fool
"Who told his baby goodbye . . ."

The stars wheeled on in heaven, and the wind bent trees toward the cold earth. Men noted the comings and goings of Marilyn Monroe, hung on every word of Rock Hudson and Doris Day, while I had become a resident of the lunatic fringe. Oh well, Marilyn and Rock had their problems, and I had mine. I liked mine better than theirs.

II

LIVING IT OUT

11

Went down to the crossroads . . .
~ Robert Johnson ~

If you come to a fork in the road, take it.
~ Yogi Berra ~

Enter ye in at the strait gate.
~ Jesus, Matt. 7: 13 ~

And so I stood at mid-century, in middle-America, at both the crossroads of the country and the crossroads of my young life. I was very much a product of the American environment as it had developed over the years. We were dream-spinners, all of us, grasping for glory and at the same time yearning backward toward the innocence of a long-lost Eden. The Republic spread out all around is, thousands of miles of highways and rutted country roads, along which the people of legend had moved, and my nameless ancestors with them.

They were Celtic peoples with leanings toward superstition and violence, who quitted the Highlands and borderlands of Scotland, and with ragged clothes on their backs and homemade fiddles under their arms they crossed the wild North Atlantic in whatever would float. Oh, and also tucked under their arms were King James Bibles. They were possessed of certain beliefs which they passed on to their children. God was watching. Good men went to heaven. Bad men went to hell. Papists, Jews and people who violated the Christian Sabbath were bad men. Hard work, honesty and thrift were characteristic behavior of the Lord's chosen people. This notion—the so-called Protestant ethic—would become deeply imbedded in the American psyche.

Off the boats they tumbled, hungry and semi-literate, to begin the westward trek, over the mountains, through the Cumberland Gap, into the trans-Appalachian areas of Kentucky and Tennessee, pausing here and there to throw up crude cabins and beget children, some of which survived infancy, then moving on down rivers named Ohio and Wabash and Mississippi into woods teaming with game and with an ancient race they called, "Them murderin' redskins." They built roaring fires that lit up the purple nights, guzzled raw whiskey, fought with fists and knives, lynched, relented, repented. Fiddles squealed, and they danced the old dances and sang the old songs from the country they'd left behind.

> Holiday, holiday, the best day of the year,
> Lord Donald's wife came into church, the
> Gospel for to hear.
> And ere the meeting had begun she cast her eyes about,
> And there she spied little Mattie Groves a walkin'
> in the crowd.

But they didn't come alone, these peripatetic dreamers. Hard on their heels and riding to keep up came a man in broadcloth with hawk's eyes and a mouth like an axe blade. The circuit rider dismounted, climbed up on a stump and announced his text. The words rushed out like the shout of Gideon's trumpet, fresh from the heart of the backwoods Homer—dark words, mighty words, words of damnation and woe, words of light and ecstasy. He was a Methodist, a Baptist, a Presbyterian, a Campbellite. And finally it didn't matter what he was, for he proclaimed the same message as all the others. It was Calvinism in a buckskin shirt, fundamentalism in a coonskin cap, literalism that smelled of woods and rivers.

Brother, the great American camp meeting was underway, a meeting destined to roll unabated across the years of the history of the Republic. Americans apparently wanted hardcore Calvinistic fundamentalism, and to this they would turn back time and time again over the years when things got tough. The fire might burn low in one place and during one generation, but all it needed was a new down-home spellbinder to blow the embers up to flame.

There's sin in the camp tonight. I say there's a great sinner here. You may believe you can hide. You hide from that dear mother who's been praying for you. You hide from that godly pastor who weeps over you. But you can't hide from God. He sees you, and He knows you. Pray, pray that by His grace you'll be spared from the fires of damnation.

And the flock waded waist deep into cold rivers and were baptized in the Name of the Father, Son and Holy Ghost while others stood on the bank holding torches and singing:

> On Jordan's stormy banks I stand,
> And cast a wistful eye
> To Canaan's fair and happy land,
> Where my possessions lie.

Jonathan Edwards held terrified New Englanders over the pits of hell and turned up the heat. The Great Awakening swept the land with the fury of a storm.

Then, when things got back to normal and people were back to sinning comfortably, onto the stage stepped Charles Finney, a New York lawyer hypnotic of eye and straight as a rail, to call down the wrath of the Almighty in a style none could gainsay. He gave lie to the old school Calvinism that said no man could choose salvation. Indeed, he said, men are called upon to repent and choose Christ. Charges of Arminianism shot from the hallowed halls of Yale and Princeton bounded off him like pebbles off steel plate. "Come down to the mourner's bench," he said. "Come down, and pray through."

The next link in the chain was a lad from Northfield, Massachusetts, who left his home and went off to Boston to seek his fortune. One day while he was working in his uncle's shoe store, Edward Kimball, a Sunday school teacher in a local Congregational Church came in to visit him and asked him if he didn't think it was time to get his life right with the Lord. The lad allowed that it was, and Dwight L. Moody was on his way.

The revival rolled on.

Moody removed himself from Boston for the more promising spaces of a rough-and-tumble town on the shores of Lake Michigan, a place called Chicago, and there he hustled shoes, led prayer meetings in the newly-founded YMCA and organized a Sunday school in a downtown slum populated by immigrants who had trouble speaking English. He went to England along with a Pennsylvania songster, Ira Sankey, and when he came back home and stepped off the boat, he found that he had become famous during his absence. He received invitations to hold meetings in Brooklyn, Philadelphia, New York. He and Sankey preached and sang the liberals out of town on the proverbial rail:

> 'Twas grace that wrote my name in life's eternal book,
> And grace that brought me to the Lamb, who all my
> sorrows took.
> Saved by grace alone, this is all my plea.
> Jesus died for all mankind, and Jesus died for me.

Meanwhile, back in Chicago, another storm was brewing. One day in the mid-1880s a handful of drunks stepped out of a saloon and saw, across the street, a gospel band from the Pacific Garden Mission. The drunks were all members of the major league baseball club known then as the Chicago White Stockings. They sat down on the curb and listened to the music. Finally a man with the band, Harry Monroe, invited the listeners to come down to the mission to hear more preaching and singing. One of the ballplayers went along because, as he later explained, the gospel songs reminded him of songs he had heard his mother singing when he was a farm boy in Iowa.

Look out, America, here comes Billy Sunday!

He was crude and vulgar, but he was eloquent, a born showman. He had a rapid-fire delivery, spitting out three hundred words a minute, and he was a flag-waving, shouting patriot who had no time for dancing, card-playing, or booze. Booze, he said, put a bullet through Lincoln and McKinley. Booze was the way the white slavers robbed 50,000 American girls of their virtue every year. But as long as he had a fist, he'd punch booze. As long as he had a foot, he'd kick it. As long as he had teeth, he'd bite it. And when he was old, and gray, and toothless, and bootless, he'd gum it. He intended to fight booze until the day he died—when he'd go home to glory, and booze would go to perdition.

He dazzled his audiences by stringing words together so rapidly that they could hardly follow him. Those ossified, petrified, mildewed, dyed-in-the-wool, stamped-in-the-cork, blown-in-the bottle, horizontal, perpendicular Presbyterians. Those red-nosed, buttermilk-eyed, beetle-browed, peanut-brained, stall-fed saloon-keepers. He turned handsprings, slid into imaginary bases, shook his fists.

The intellectuals shuddered with horror. But the people loved Billy Sunday. Then the machinery wound down, and he gave up the ghost—but not before he had ventured into the hill country of North Carolina to hold a meeting that stirred up the folks for years to come. It stirred them so deeply, in fact, that during the Great Depression some men, longing for another revival of the old time religion, decided to get together for a day of prayer.

They met on the farm of one of the locals, down in a wooded area where they knelt down on pine needles. They fasted and prayed all day, rough men in brogans and overalls, down on their knees under the pines, beseeching God to send a revival.

Across the road in a field two men were working. One was a hired man, the other was the son of the man who owned the farm. They saw the supplicants coming and going.

"Who are them men?" the hired man asked.

"I don't know," the boy replied. "I guess some fanatics that talked dad into letting them use the place."

One of the fanatics prayed that God be pleased to raise up from among them one who would take the Gospel to the ends of the earth. And God did just that. He took the lad who had seen the praying men as a bunch of fanatics, and He sent him out to the ends of the earth to proclaim the Good News about Jesus Christ. But more importantly, from my point of view, He sent the North Carolina preacher boy, Billy Graham, to Oklahoma City in the summer of 1956, and the preacher boy gave out the Gospel as he had been sent to do, and Mike Davis got saved, and indirectly, so did I.

This brings me back to my opening statement. I stood at mid-century, very much a product of my environment. Racially, I was German and Scots-Irish. A southern American up from the East Texas cotton fields, I represented the first generation of my line to grow up in urban America. We were not poor, but we were not rich either. We believed implicitly in the American dream. It would never have occurred to any of us to burn his draft card or to refuse to salute the American flag. We stood up and placed our hands over our hearts when a band played the "Star-Spangled Banner."

I say all of this not because it is good. Nor do I say it because it is bad. I say it because that is the way we were.

We did not have television sets for the first ten or eleven years of my existence. We listened to the radio and shared the hopes and dreams of Stella Dallas, Helen Trent, and Ma Perkins. We danced to the music of Guy Lombardo and Artie Shaw and Glenn Miller, until a more primitive and joyous beat emerged from the other side of the tracks to engage our interest.

Aside from their music, we had little connection with those widely referred to as "colored people." It never occurred to us to ask whether they were happy or sad. They must have been happy; they were always singing and dancing and clowning around.

We spent our summers in the minor league ball park watching our Double-A Texas League team and yelling like savages. Or, we went to the movies, paid a dime to get in, and thrilled to the exploits of Hoot Gibson and Ken Maynard.

To say that we were naïve is a colossal understatement.

But if this all sounds ordinary enough, my spiritual pedigree does not. For I was a direct descendent of the great evangelicals who so imprinted themselves upon our culture. I knew none of this when I was first saved, but in short order I found that I was very much like them. I was a semi-Calvinist, who held to the fundamentals of the Christian Faith, possessed of a conviction that it was my duty to spread the Gospel to the ends of the earth. I guess, now that I think about it, that I had become another Jim McIntyre. We were brothers, born of a common parent.

12

Don't know much about history.
~ Sam Cooke ~

Study to shew thyself approved unto God,
a workman that needeth not to be ashamed,
rightly dividing the Word of truth.
~ Paul to Timothy (II Tim. 2:15) ~

"Okay, you've got a bunch of Christians in Rome, a bunch of Gentiles . . ."

Four of us—Bill Sam Knight, Joe Hanks, McIntyre and I—sat in Jim McIntyre's living room. We had our Bibles opened, with pads and pencils handy, ready to take notes. It was Saturday morning, sometime in mid-March, 1957. McIntyre's wife, a tall Swede named Mary, was there too, but she was sort of in and out, running after their two kids and cleaning up messes.

"So Paul is over in Corinth . . ."

"Wait a minute," I said. I was the most scripturally ignorant of the group by a considerable measure. "How do we know he was in Corinth?"

"Because of the way he ended the letter," said McIntyre. "He says he is staying in the home of Gauis. And we can read his letter to the Corinthians and learn that Gaius lived in Corinth."

"Okay."

"Got it?"

"Yeah."

"So in Gaius's home there is a slave named Tertius, and Paul dictates the letter to him, and Tertius signs himself at the end. Tertius means three."

"That's a weird name," Joe Hanks said.

"Not for a Greek slave," said McIntyre. "Back in those days they used to take away slave's names and give them numbers."

"So this guy Gaius owned slaves," I said.

"Ah," McIntyre said, "that's the beauty of it. These men were Christian. On one level they were slave and master, but on a more important level they were brothers in the Lord. One of them calls himself, 'Quartus, a brother.' Quartus means four. But he's one of the brotherhood, and that makes all the difference."

"That's neat," Bill Sam said.

"Yeah, that is neat," I said.

"Because that's how it is with those who know the Lord." McIntyre paused, seemed to be looking at something far away. "Look at the four of us," he went on. "We hardly have anything in common from the world's point of view. We probably would never gravitate toward each other naturally. But we share a common life in the Lord, and we are really closer than blood brothers."

"Really neat," said Bill Sam.

"But why are we reading *Romans*?" I asked. "You told me to read *Romans*. I never read the Bible before. But I just figured to start on page one and go through to the end."

"*Romans* is basic," Joe Hanks said.

"That's right," said McIntyre. "To miss *Romans* is to miss what Christianity is all about. Christianity is not religion, not in the strictest sense. Religion, any religion, is a human system that is supposed to get you to God. You get in the system and follow a bunch of rules and regulations. Christianity is a relationship with Jesus Christ."

"Boy, you lost me somewhere," I said.

"That's why we're going through *Romans*. When we get through, your life will never be the same. You'll see everything in a different light."

"Keep talking," Joe Hanks said. "I'll take all the new light I can get."

"Okay. You'll notice that the book falls into certain divisions. Paul begins by talking about how the Gospel is the power of God unto salvation. Then he starts making a case against mankind. He's like a prosecuting attorney in a court of law. He starts his case by showing that all men are lost. Not just ignorant savages, but educated men, even very religious men. Religion never saved anyone. His conclusion to the argument is found in chapter 3, verse 23: 'All have sinned and come short of the glory of God.'"

"Do you suppose my preacher is lost?" I asked.

"Well, let's put it this way," McIntyre answered, "being a preacher won't save you."

"I used to think that being a preacher was a sure ticket to heaven."

Joe Hanks laughed. "So did I," he said.

"The sure ticket to heaven," McIntyre said, "is seen in the very next verse, verse 24. If Paul has made his case, if all men are lost, then is that the end of the matter? And if not, then how are they to be saved? They can't try religion. Paul already proved in his argument that religion won't work."

"Where does he say that?" I asked. I must have seemed monumentally stupid to the others.

"All over chapter 3," said Bill Sam.

"Right," McIntyre said. "That's what he's talking about in his statement to the Jews. If religion could make a man right with God, then the Jews would have been the rightest of the right. They had God's Law, delivered to Moses and brought down from the mountain. But Paul concludes that they are no better off than the gentiles, who never had the Law. The Law did nothing but condemn them, because having the Law and keeping the Law are two different things. They had the Law, but they never kept it."

"No one could keep a law like that," Joe Hanks said.

"Exactly the point," McIntyre said. "The Law hung around their necks like a millstone. It should have driven them to God for mercy. All have sinned and come short of the glory of God. So men don't need justice; they need mercy. They need free justification. And that's where Romans 3:24 comes in. Justification is free, by God's grace, through faith in Jesus Christ."

"What is this grace?" I asked.

"Well," McIntyre said, "look at the verse. He says we are justified freely. That word 'freely' is the same word used by the Lord in the

Gospel of John when he said, 'They hated me *without a cause.*' There was no cause for God's loving us, anymore than there was a cause for their hating His Son. The cause for their hate is found within themselves, not in the One they hate. And the cause for His loving us is found in Him, not in us."

"It's kind of humbling, ain't it?" Bill Sam said.

"Yeah," I said. "Kind of."

"To think that I'm not naturally lovable."

"My mother thinks I'm naturally lovable," Joe Hanks said.

"Your mother doesn't know you as well as God does," McIntyre said.

We all laughed. Mary brought in hot chocolate, and we sat in the living room sipping and talking and laughing, learning what we were in Christ. My ignorance was not to be taken, according to McIntyre, as evidence of not being saved. Rather, I was like a newborn babe. I had new and eternal life, now I was involved in a sort of spiritual odyssey. I would spend the rest of my earthly experience on my road home finding out who and what I had become spiritually.

At about noon a car pulled up at the front curb. We heard the engine gun, then shut down. Joe Hanks looked out through the living room's large front window. "An old car," he said. "Looks like a forty-one Ford. You know anyone who drives a forty-one Ford, McIntyre?"

"Nope."

"You know a woman who's wider than she is tall?"

"Hey," I said, "it's Ellie Wassom and Mike Davis. I told them we were getting together today. I've been wanting them to meet you, McIntyre."

The day was raw and windy. Mike leaned into the wind as he crossed the lawn up to McIntyre's porch. The wind didn't bother Ellie at all. Nothing short of a hurricane could have moved her. She had a purse hooked over her right arm and a broad hat on her head, and with her left hand she held her hat on her head. She looked like an early and heavier version of Bella Abzug.

"Boy," Davis said as he burst through the front door, "if I had wings I could fly. Who ordered up all this wind?"

"He that troubleth his own house shall inherit the wind," McIntyre intoned.

"I troubled my house just this morning," Davis said. "Got into a knock-down-drag-out with my mom."

"Well, there you go," Ellie said, having gotten inside. "I'd suggest you go home and apologize."

"Ellie, I'm Jim McIntyre."

"I remember you," Ellie said. "You played basketball once in Sioux Falls when I was there." She shifted her purse to her left arm, extended her right hand and said, "But I never thought I'd actually get a chance to meet you."

As we stood there, with introductions going back and forth, it occurred to me that we were by all odds a motley looking crew: McIntyre, towering over us; Ellie rotund and peering through thick glasses; four kids in blue jeans and sneakers; Mary and her hyperactive children. And now that I sit here writing, years after the fact, I marvel at the way the Lord works and the ones He chooses to work through. Not many mighty, not many noble, not many wise, but the weak, the ignoble, the foolish are chosen to confound the great men of the world, that no flesh may glory in His presence.

We situated ourselves on the available furniture, and Mary hauled in more hot chocolate.

"When people start getting saved, my adrenalin starts to flow," Ellie said. "I believe the Lord is doing something important, and we're right in the middle of it."

"What do you think He's doing?" McIntyre asked.

"I think a bunch of kids are about to find out that Jesus Christ is something other than a picture on a wall. I think we're going to see revival break out, just like in the days of Jonathan Edwards."

"We already are," McIntyre said. "Billy Graham stirred it up when he was here. It's just the beginning."

"Maybe it's Billy," Ellie replied. "But for sure it's the Lord. Just between us, I've always been a little skeptical about big time revivalism. I've seen revival before. I never saw it going on in tent meetings. It's always been in living rooms, just like this, with people and open Bibles."

"So what do you intend to do?" McIntyre asked.

"Nothing, really," Ellie told him. "There's nothing I can do. Just be there. We've got a prayer meeting going on Thursday nights. Just started it. Had our first meeting Thursday over at Nancy McNatt's place. Fifty kids showed up. Not an adult in the group. And these were kids I never see in church. The Classen High School crowd."

"I'm telling you, it was great!" Mike Davis said.

"What did you do?" I asked.

"We talked."

"Talked?" It was Bill Sam Knight, slightly bewildered.

"Mike started talking about how the Lord had changed his life," said Ellie. "Then Billy Reynolds. Then a bunch of the kids started asking questions. So we got out what Bibles we had and started answering them. Then we prayed."

"Prayed?" I said.

"Not all of us," Mike said. "Ellie asked Billy Reynolds to pray, and I thought, 'Oh, no, not Billy.' Man, you should have heard his prayer. It sent cold chills up my back. That guy was really talking to the Lord. Then I prayed. Then this guy from school, this football player named Jess Farley, prayed. I never thought old Jess had a decent bone in his body. But he started praying. Then, you know what? He started crying. Then I started crying."

We sat in McIntyre's living room, stunned into silence. Even McIntyre's kids quieted down, and Mary came in and sat with us. We found ourselves swept up in something none of us, not even McIntyre, understood—the ignition of a roaring conflagration that no man could begin or end.

"Good grief," McIntyre whispered. "I've heard of things like this, but I never thought I'd see one. I heard of a revival breaking out on a college campus, and people would simply walk onto the campus and fall down and get saved."

"It happened in New England with Jonathan Edwards," Ellie said. "Entire towns were saved. Saloons and theaters shut down. All people talked about was the Lord. I'm telling you, this is revival, an awakening of the Spirit. We've got to pray—for all we're worth. Who knows where it might lead?"

"We need to get a prayer meeting started in Putnam City," said Joe Hanks.

"But who would come?" I asked. "I tried to tell some of the guys about the Lord, and all they did was laugh. I'd like to see old Joe Ed Tracy praying and crying."

"Revival isn't something you can just start," Ellie said. "If the Lord's in it, it'll go, and no man can stop it. If the Lord's not in it, you can do what you will, and it'll fall flatter than a pancake."

"Let's pray for Putnam City High School," said McIntyre. "Let's ask the Lord to do here what He's doing at Classen."

And we did. We got down on our knees (except for Ellie), and we asked the Lord to send us an awakening.

13

I'm not gonna get up there and make a sap of myself.
~ Dawson Trotman, in his testimony ~

I am not ashamed of the gospel of Christ.
~ The Apostle Paul, Romans 1:16 ~

By now the whole school knew that I had been saved, or hit the sawdust trail, or got religion, or turned over a new leaf, or whatever they called it. And most knew that this wasn't just a passing fancy—at least they thought it seemed real enough. But they didn't like it very well. It was as if I had come down with some peculiar affliction and had been put in quarantine so as not to infect others. I would come upon groups of guys talking, and they would immediately change the subject. Or they'd get mad at something and swear, and then they'd apologize and grin like fools.

The coaches were perhaps the most baffled of the bunch. Their team captain had publicly declared for Christ, and they didn't know what this could possibly mean. No doubt I would be turning the other cheek to irreligious opponents and be ground into ignominy, taking the rest of the team with me.

"Well," the basketball coach said, "it doesn't seem to have affected his basketball playing. He can still dribble the ball and shoot."

"We'll see next fall if he can still knock people down and step on them," one of the football coaches said.

And there was poor, bewildered Connie Mason, still hovering around hoping I would come to my senses, but seeing little chance of it the longer I pursued whatever will-o'-the-wisp had beguiled me.

But my teachers and schoolmates had no idea what was just around the corner—nor did I.

Remember the speech class I had with Mrs. Wood? Well, I still had it, and I still made rotten speeches, even if I now tried a little harder. Anyway, one day not long after the Saturday get-together in McIntyre's home, Mrs. Wood approached me in the hall outside her classroom and said:

"Mrs. Smith asked me if I would let you come down to her typing class and speak."

"Do what?" I said.

"Mrs. Smith is a very religious woman." Mrs. Wood smiled as if discussing a quaint curiosity. "She wants you to come and give a speech to her typing class about your . . . ah . . . experience. I told her I'd ask you if you would, but that I wouldn't make you."

"You want me to?"

She shrugged. "It's up to you. But if you give a speech, for heaven's sake act like I've taught you something. Remember what Mark Twain said. Tell 'em what you're gonna tell 'em. Tell 'em. Then tell 'em what you told 'em. Don't stand up there like a post. Be animated. And keep your eyes moving over your audience."

"I'm supposed to go down there and preach?"

"You don't have to."

I could think of many reasons not to go. I could think of only one reason why I should, a Bible verse I had read only recently: *Let the redeemed of the Lord say so.*

"Are you going with me?"

"Not me," Mrs. Wood said. "I have a class to teach. Besides, she wants to hear from you, not me."

She began picking at my shirt. "Straighten up your collar, now, and pull up your pants a little. You don't want to go in there looking like something the cat dragged in."

She seemed so maternal, as if she was worried to death I would make a public spectacle of myself. And, of course, I had the same concern.

"Okay," I said, "I'm going."

"Do good."

"Mrs. Wood, I'm sure that I'll be run out of school. I think I'll just make the speech, then walk out the door and keep going."

"You'll do fine," she said. "Just keep your head. And spit out that gum!"

I walked down the hall on wobbly legs, my heart pounding away, a nervous wreck. I didn't know how much worse I could have felt if I were going before a firing squad. It was a fine kettle of fish I had gotten myself into. Already I was the subject of ridicule and gossip (at least I imagined I was), and this would be the final blow, the *coup de grace* to a waning career.

I came to Mrs. Smith's room, stood outside the door, and sucked air into my lungs. "Oh, Lord," I prayed, "get me out of this in one piece, and I'll never ask you for another thing."

I pushed the door open and walked in.

Typewriters clacked away as students bent to their work. Mrs. Smith sat at her desk at the front of the room. Some of the students looked up. Some did not.

"Mrs. Smith," I whispered, "Mrs. Wood told me I was supposed to come and make a speech for you."

"Well, I asked her if you would."

"Okay. Well . . ."

"Are you ready?"

"I guess so. What do you want me to say?"

"Why, everyone says you got saved. I think that's wonderful. I'd like for you to tell these young people about it."

"Do they know I'm going to talk?"

"No, because I wasn't sure you would. But if you're ready, I'll introduce you."

"Go ahead," I said. And I thought, *let's get this over with.*

"Everybody," she said. "Stop typing and give me your attention. Doug has something to say."

Just like that. Doug has something to say. She sat back down. The room got quiet. It seemed a long time before I could get my tongue to work. Most of the students were girls, though there were a few boys in the room. Dark-eyed Abby French was there, and Charlene Hardison, and way in the back of the room, wearing my letter jacket, which she kept threatening to give back but never had, sat Connie Mason.

"Mrs. Wood sent me down here," I said. "She said that Mrs. Smith asked me to come. She said Mrs. Smith is a very religious woman, and that she wanted me to come down and talk about my experience with the Lord."

The room got deathly quiet. Abby French's lips parted, and she riveted her dark eyes on me. Connie Mason looked as if she would faint and fall sideways out of her chair.

"I'm not very religious," I said. "I never was. I went to church, but I never knew much about religion. I just thought that you should be as good as you could be, and that if you were, you would be all right with the Lord. Then something happened. I went home one rainy night, and my father told me that Rusty Borden had been struck by lightning and killed. I was very upset about that. I guess we all were. But I kept wondering where Rusty is now, and what he's doing, and what it's like to die.

"Then I started wondering why he had died instead of me. And I knew that I had to die someday too. It was just a matter of time. I started having trouble sleeping at night. I know that none of you knew that, because I covered it up. Here I was, hotshot jock, afraid to die.

"So I tried to figure out why I felt that way, and all I could come up with was that I was no good. I felt like I needed to change my life and get right with God. But I didn't know how. I tried to be good, but I couldn't do it.

"Then Billy Graham came to town and a friend of mine named Mike Davis got saved. And he started telling me that you couldn't be good enough to work your way to heaven. He said that what I needed was to have my sins forgiven, and that Jesus, God's Son, had died for my sins. What I had to do was believe in Him and receive Him as my savior. But I didn't know what that meant. I thought I believed all this, but I knew that I wasn't saved.

"Then one Sunday night not long ago the Lord saved me. It's kind of hard to explain. But it's like you're in a dark room and suddenly light shines in. It's like you have a blindfold on, and suddenly someone takes it off. I knew that everything I had ever heard about Jesus is true. He is just who He said He was, and He died for me, just like I always heard He had. And the resurrection . . . it's all true.

"So I got saved. And I told my friends. And they said, 'That's great,' but they didn't get saved. And most of them don't want to talk about the Lord. That makes me sad, because this is the most fantastic experience I've ever had. And people say, 'Yeah, that's great,' and walk away.

"But I'd rather be saved than anything. To be the captain of the football team, and to be lost . . . What will it matter in the long run if we never even have a football team?

"Well, that's about it. I'm not the same guy I was. Don't expect me to be."

They all sat stiff as boards and looked at me. I started backing toward the door, not a very graceful exit, but the best I could come up with.

"Thank you, Doug," I heard Mrs. Smith say.

"You're welcome," I heard myself reply.

A few typewriters had already begun to clatter as I eased out the door and closed it behind me. I exhaled, my heart still pounding away, and started back to Mrs. Wood's class. Then I heard the door to Mrs. Smith's room open and close, and footsteps, clearly feminine, rapidly overtaking me.

"Doug, wait . . ."

It was Abby French, dark-eyed Abby, who would cry at a moment's notice. I stopped, turned back, and, yes, she was crying.

"I have to talk to you," she said. "I'm just like you were. I'm lost and I don't know how to be saved."

An interesting predicament. Before me stood a girl who wanted to be saved because of what she had heard me say, and I didn't know what to tell her. In a flash I recalled the time I sat with Mike Davis in his old Mercury and we talked about being saved, and I had no idea how to go about it. I recalled the times McIntyre had talked to me and how I had given intellectual assent to the truth of everything he said, then walked away as lost as ever.

"Abby," I said, "Jesus died for you."

"I know that," she said, "but I don't know how to be saved."

"You have to trust in Him." I began fishing around for something else to say because she stood there looking at me as if she and I occupied opposite corners of the universe. "He said," I finally told her, 'He that cometh to me I will in no wise cast out.'"

"He said that?"

"Yes."

"And how do I come to Him?"

"Why you just . . . you just come to Him, right here. You take Him as your Savior."

"Just like that?"

"Yes, because you believe in Him, you believe that He can save you."

She had begun to sob as if in mortal agony, and she fled down the hallway toward the gymnasium. I had no idea what she expected to find there.

By now Mrs. Smith had come into the hall looking for Abby. She rushed up to me, her heels clicking on the floor beneath her.

"What is the matter with that girl?" she demanded. "The minute you left she started crying and ran out of the room."

"I guess I upset her," I said. "I didn't mean to."

"Where did she go?"

I nodded toward the gym.

Mrs. Smith, frowning, said, "Go on to class. I'll go and get her."

I thought I should go too, but because I didn't know what I would do for poor Abby if I found her, I shrugged and walked away.

In what must have been record time word of this incident spread all over school, and to the epithets already tagged onto me, some new ones were added. I was a preacher, a wild-eyed revivalist, Putnam City's answer to Gypsy Smith.

That night, after we had eaten supper and I sat in my room half-heartedly doing my homework, the phone rang. It was Abby French.

"Doug, can you come over?"

"You mean right now?"

"Yes. I have to talk to you. And Joe Ed is here. And my mother and father. And Charlene is here too."

"Well, Abby, I . . ."

"Doug, I *have* to talk to you."

"Abby, I have to write this English paper . . ."

"It won't take long . . ."

"Okay, I'm on my way."

This optimistic statement, uttered before I checked with my parents, almost foundered on the rocks of hard reality. Mom insisted I finish my homework, and dad, for reasons best known to him, didn't want to let me have the car. Abby lived over a mile away, so the idea of walking there and back on a dark, cold night didn't excite much enthusiasm in me. But I finally managed to beg and cajole my way out of the house with the car keys in hand, and off I went.

Over at the French place I found a scene that must have been similar, on a small scale, to that which greeted Simon Peter when he entered the home of Cornelius the Centurion. There they all sat: Mr. French on the sofa with a martini glass in hand; Mrs. French beside him, hands folded in lap, very serene and refined; Joe Ed slumped in an easy chair, either angry or sick; Charlene, in blue jeans with her shirt tale out, cross-legged on the floor; Abby, also in blue jeans, down there with Charlene. There was another lady there too. She actually answered the door when I rang the bell and ushered me in. But she turned out to be a neighbor who had come over to borrow something, and she didn't stay around long.

"Well, come in son, come in." Mr. French rose up, martini glass in his left hand, extending his right.

I crossed the room and shook his hand. He was quite drunk, or else he just naturally slurred his words and had red eyes.

"Sit down where you can find a place," he said, and he plopped back down beside his wife.

A straight-backed chair of the cane-bottom variety, very out of place in this upper middle-class environment, sat conspicuously empty beside Joe Ed. I took it, apprehensive and tightly coiled.

"How ya doin', Joe Ed?"

"I don't know," he said. "Either I'm going nuts or everyone else is."

"What do you mean?"

"Ask Abby."

I looked to Abby.

"I'm saved," she said. "I got saved today."

"How?" I asked.

"That's what I'd like to know," said Mr. French. "What is all this 'saved' business?"

Mr. French was what I would now call typical of his generation, and of the fifties fathers, perhaps the first to really experience a yawning generation gap that would widen into a chasm in the sixties. He had come out of the Depression with little more than pocket change and a used suit of clothes, had gone off to fight in France, had come back to greet his wife and a daughter he hardly knew, had finished college on the G.I. Bill, had made lots of money as a corporate executive—and consumed large amounts of gin and vermouth when he came home in the evening.

"Come on now, son, I want to hear about this business of being saved. Abby's bouncing off the walls . . ."

"Daddy!"

"Saved from what?"

There he sat, he and his wife, looking at me. In fact, they were all looking at me, waiting for an answer to one of the most basic questions anyone can ask: saved from what?

I was no theologian, nor did I have a sound knowledge of the Bible. I knew little more than my own experience, so I started from the beginning, the death of Rusty Borden, and I talked about what had happened to me. As I talked, I warmed to the subject. My fear and uneasiness went away. I could tell that they were listening, that they were caught up in the story as it unfolded. I was very like the man in the ninth chapter of John's Gospel: *Whether He be a sinner or no, I know not; one thing I know, whereas I was blind, now I see.*

"You've got lots of guts, kid," Mr. French said when I finally quit talking. "I sure don't think you're going to win a popularity contest. But I don't imagine too many people will care to argue with the captain of the football team."

We were quiet for a moment. Then Mr. French said, "You really believe all this, huh?"

"Yes, I do," I said.

"We used to go to church," Mrs. French wistfully muttered. "When Abby was little. Maybe we should start again."

"No," Mr. French said. "I'm too old for that. But if Abby wants to go . . ."

"You're not too old, Daddy," Abby said.

I turned to Joe Ed. "What about you, buddy. Are you too old, or too tough?"

"Lay off," he growled. "I don't want any part of this salvation stuff."

Abby acted as if she hadn't heard Joe Ed. She was talking to me. "It was when you said, 'He that cometh to Me I will in no wise cast out.' When you said that, I thought, 'That means me.'"

"But what does that mean?" Mr. French asked.

"It means what it says," I replied.

"But I know how to go to Joe Ed. I just get up and walk across the room. How do I come to someone who is invisible, who is nowhere?"

"You mean everywhere," Abby said.

Charlene Hardison, silent up to now, asked a question worthy of a philosopher: "But everywhere, that's sort of the same as nowhere—isn't it?"

"He's here," I said. "Right now. You can come to Him right now if you want to."

"But what if I don't want to?" asked Joe Ed, and quickly followed with, "Which I don't."

I shrugged. "Then you won't," I said. "But if you don't, you're lost. And why would you want to be lost?"

"Because I don't believe any of this."

"I don't know if I believe it or not," Mr. French said, and drained off about half of his martini in one gulp. "I remember when we went ashore at Normandy. Omaha Beach. I was in the first wave on D-Day. I spent the whole day in a hole with my face in the sand, scared out of my wits. I must have seen a hundred men blown to bits. I told the Lord if He'd get me out alive, I'd do whatever He wanted me to. I did nothing. I never have done anything. I think it's too late for me."

"I don't think it is," I said. "I think you can still keep that promise."

It got quiet again.

"I've got to go home," I said. "Homework."

"Come back," said Mrs. French.

"Yes, do," Abby said.

I got up and started for the door. To my surprise, Joe Ed followed me out. When we got to my car, he said:

"Look, man, I've been pretty rotten. What you're doing is okay. I just don't understand it. I don't understand what's happened to

Abby. And her old man . . . A good old boy, but a lush. Now there he sits talking about his duty to God. I don't understand any of it."

"Get saved," I said. "Then you'll understand it."

"Sure, and be put down as a grade-A nut."

"Like me?"

"Yeah, man, just like you."

He threw back his head and laughed. I laughed with him.

The next morning in school I got two surprises. The first was when I walked through the front door and a girl from the office handed me a note.

"It's from a guy named Mike Davis," she said. "He called and said to give you this message—said it was a matter of life and death."

The note said I had to come to the Classen High School prayer meeting that night. He wanted me to speak. It was to be at his house, and they expected to have seventy-five kids out.

The second surprise came when I saw Joe Ed talking to one of the football players, Dave Winchell. Joe Ed had, of all things, a pocket New Testament and was showing Dave something, or trying to.

"Hey, Miller," he said, "come here. That bit about not casting out whoever comes to Him . . . Where is that?"

A lump rose up in my throat. I almost started bawling like Abby French. I took the New Testament from him and turned to the *Gospel of John.*

14

As soon as they were come to land,
they saw a fire of coals there,
and fish laid thereon, and bread
~ John 21:9 ~

Come ye yourselves apart into a desert place,
and rest awhile
~ Mark 6:31 ~

Like it or not (and many did not like it), the Awakening was under way, as Ellie had predicted, completely out of human hands, and we were caught up in the very middle of it. And that was why, among other reasons, we all climbed into a variety of cars one Friday afternoon and headed for Devil's Canyon.

Devil's Canyon was a camp ground in a rugged area south of Clinton. There were cabins there, and a big lodge, a creek full of water, trees and sheer sandstone cliffs that rose fifty feet above the canyon floor. Ellie, in a moment of inspiration, got the church to rent the grounds for a weekend retreat. The turnout was tremendous. In fact we had to quit inviting people when the number of attendees exceeded the camp's capacity.

The Classen High School crowd came out in force. The Awakening had swept the student body there top to bottom. Putnam City was more modestly represented, but it was interesting to see who opted for a weekend with the religious nuts. Bill Sam Knight and Joe Hanks went along, and Jim McIntyre with them. Abby French came, as did Charlene Hardison, and amazingly they dragged Joe Ed Tracy and Dave Winchell with them. Joe Ed protested that he was going only because it was free and he needed to get out of town for awhile. But the most unexpected participant, from my point of view, was Connie Mason.

I had begun to have serious doubts about Connie's stated hostility to the Gospel. What she kept saying and what she kept doing were two different things. She wanted no part of Jesus Christ or salvation, as she never tired of declaring, but she continued flitting about the fringes of the inner group of believers. She fashioned a purely secular reason for going down to Devil's Canyon, as had Joe Ed. She said her friends were going. That was it, pure and simple. But I could sense a real spiritual hunger in her, though I am hard-pressed these many years later to say exactly how she communicated this. Perhaps it was through the hostility itself. Mention Jesus Christ to her and she started squirming like a trapped animal, and her eyes lit up like a forest fire. Had she been indifferent and laughed the matter off, I would have no reason, viewing it in retrospect, to feel that she was a hooked fish trying to fight back to open sea.

Anyway, we started off on a Friday afternoon. Jim McIntyre drove, and Ellie in her '41 Ford she called Myrtle Belle. Davis drove his '53 Mercury, and Dave Winchell drove his Chevy with the pin-striping. The Classen crowd had rolling stock of various ages and descriptions. I went with Connie in her Jeep. It was an interesting vehicle, salvaged from the Second World War and painted orange. It had no top. She kept it parked under a carport at her home, and her great fear, as she expressed it that afternoon, was that it would rain on us. Her concern must have been for herself, for the rain could hardly have hurt me or the Jeep. Her second great concern was my driving ability. She was convinced that I would run us into a tree, or a ditch, or an abutment. She was such a consummate back-seat driver that after we had gone a few miles I pulled over, yielded the driver's position to her and allowed myself to be chauffeured the rest of the way.

It rained.

West of El Reno the clouds started rolling in. By the time we had reached Hinton Junction and headed south for the canyon, we were in the middle of a bona-fide downpour. Davis passed us in his Mercury. The window on the passenger side rolled down, and smart remarks flew. Ellie passed us and honked, and her riders favored us with more smart remarks. Connie's language was definitely unbecoming.

We reached the lodge with our clothes plastered to us and Connie's hair hanging straight down like wet hay, and we parked her Jeep beneath the relative shelter of a large oak and made a run for it. We burst into the lodge, and a great cheer went up. Most of the others had arrived ahead of us.

"Just a-walking in the rain . . ." Joe Ed crooned.

Connie stuck her tongue out at him.

"Come over to the fire and dry out," Ellie said. "You'll both catch cold."

"No problem," Connie replied. "In an outfit like this I'm sure there are one or two faith-healers."

"That's called the laying on of hands," Dave Winchell said.

"My specialty," said one of the Classen boys.

"That is tacky," Abby French said.

A fire crackled away in the fireplace, casting tawny light into the room. The smell of burning oak danced around us in benevolent waves.

"You two need to get into some dry clothes," Ellie said.

Everything I had was soaked, so I borrowed a pair of pants from Mike Davis and a shirt from Billy Reynolds. The shirt was too small and the pants too big, and I could hardly borrow dry underwear. It was great fun. Connie borrowed what she could. We hung our wet things in the kitchen.

By now the others were in, and we started roasting hotdogs and marshmallows. Bill Sam Knight was, it turned out, a shade this side of being a virtuoso with a guitar, and he just happened to have one with him. He didn't need much urging to get it out and strum up a song or two. He tried his hand at a little Elvis Presley and Carl Perkins, and we were all rocking along fine and enjoying the food. Then Jim McIntyre got us channeled into a spiritual vein. "Man of Sorrows," we sang, "what a name for the Son of God who came, ruined sinners to reclaim. Hallelujah! What a Savior!"

Rain beat on the roof above us and thunder rumbled in the heaven. Someone threw some more wood on the fire. Flames licked up the chimney. We crowded into a semi-circle facing the fire, some on chairs, some on the floor, and sang the old songs of the faith passed down to us by our fathers. "Let those refuse to sing who never knew our God, but children of the heavenly King may speak their joys abroad. We're marching to Zion . . ." I watched faces of kids I had known a good part of my young life—Nancy McNatt and Billy Reynolds, Mike Davis, even Joe Ed Tracy and Connie Mason. I knew them, and yet I didn't know them. Something had happened to them all. They had stepped through some invisible portal and out into eternity, and their faces looked (I know it sounds corny) like the faces of angels, burnished gold by the firelight.

> Blessed assurance, Jesus is mine.
> Oh, what a foretaste of glory divine!
> Heir of salvation, purchase of God.
> Born of His Spirit. Washed in His blood.

Without being asked or introduced, Jim McIntyre stood up, began reading from a New Testament and then began to speak. I cannot now remember what he talked about; I only remember that there was power in what he said, and that a great solemnity fell upon us. There was a sense of the presence of the Lord, a certainty that eternal issues were being proclaimed, eternal lines drawn. The rain came down, and we sang:

> Oh do not let the word depart,
> And close thine eyes against the light.
> Dear sinner, harden not thy heart.
> Thou wouldst be saved? Why not tonight?

The sad thing is that a time such as this ever has to end. But the world crowds in on us, and the things of the world clamor for attention at all times. Just as we seemed set to continue in our mood of spiritual intensity for the rest of our lives, the door to the lodge swung open, and out of the rainy night stepped the Reverend Smith. His name was not Smith, but I'll call him that to avoid complications. He was our new preacher. The sad old man who had officiated at the service when I was saved had been run off by a congregation that could no longer abide his ineffectual bungling of the ministry, and in his place we got the Reverend Smith, a slick, young seminarian who had style and class and . . . whatever.

"Welcome, Reverend Smith," Ellie said. "Come in."

After all, since Ellie worked for him as his youth director and since the outing was being held under the auspices of his church, she had felt it only good form to ask him to come along and give us a word. While she and I never discussed the matter, I feel certain we could have agreed we would all have been better off if Reverend Smith had stayed a long way away.

Reverend Smith was a delightful, pleasant man, but he came in on the heels of Jim McIntyre's potent spiritual address, and he stood up there babbling about love and the milk of human kindness. It was perfectly obvious to all of us that Reverend Smith and Jim McIntyre stood poles apart. Jesus was someone McIntyre knew, whereas He was someone Reverend Smith knew *about.*

Then I leaped headfirst into the fray.

I don't know how the subject arose, but in some inexplicable way Reverend Smith and I became entangled in an argument over the blood atonement. He was a theologian; I was not. I took the Bible literally; he did not.

"But it says in Hebrews that without the shedding of blood there is no remission of sins."

"Yes," the Reverend countered. "But that is purely figurative. That sort of symbolism is what we would expect from men who had come out of a culture that practiced blood sacrifice. The shedding of blood meant only the giving of one's life."

"Then why was Jesus crucified?" I asked. "What if he had been strangled, or poisoned like Socrates? Would that have paid the penalty for my sins?"

"Once again, you have to understand that the biblical language is highly figurative. Jesus didn't actually bear your sins."

"Wait a minute! Give me that again. He didn't bear my sins?"

"Not literally, no."

"Then I have to bear my own."

"Well . . . yes, strictly speaking."

"And that leaves me looking forward to a one-way trip to hell."

"Doug, I hate to sound like a broken record, but you have got to develop the critical intelligence to distinguish between poetic hyperbole and fact. The hell that preachers used to shout about is pure fancy."

"Maybe heaven is pure fancy too." He was making me mad, and Ellie sensed it, got between us and invited everyone to come back to the fire and sing some more, which we did. But it wasn't the same after that, and when Reverend Smith took his leave to get back to Oklahoma City and prepare his Sunday sermon, we all felt better.

Later, after the singing stopped and the last drop of hot chocolate disappeared from the pots, most of the kids drifted away to cabins. The rain had become a mere whisper on the roof above us by now, and outside the wind picked up a bit, rattling the tree limbs and whistling against the windows. Mike Davis and I sat on wooden chairs before the great fireplace, leaning forward, elbows on knees, staring at the embers of the fire that had been. One intact log still glowed and smoldered, issuing up wisps of smoke. To our left, on the building's west end, a door opened into the kitchen, and a bar of light issued out into the cavernous darkness of the room. Ellie and several of the girls were in there cleaning up. They laughed and giggled. Connie was not with them. I had seen her leave by herself, and I wondered how all this had affected her, if at all. How, I wondered, had someone so young become so hardened against the Gospel so early? I might have answered the question by considering what I had been only a few weeks before, but self-examination wasn't one of the cards in my deck. I always found it easier to see other people's problems than to deal with my own.

"You all right?" Mike asked.

"Yeah," I said, still concentrating on the smoldering log. "I guess so."

"Boy, that guy Smith sure knows how to ruin a party, doesn't he? The fire was roaring, and he comes in with a bucket of cold water."

"I wasn't really thinking about him."

"What then?"

"Connie Mason."

"Brother, she's good looking."

"Yeah," I said, "and lost as a goose. I was watching her face tonight. She looked like she was near mental collapse. I think if someone had pointed a finger at her, she would have started screaming."

Mike nodded. "But look at it from her point of view. She's ringed in by a bunch of fanatics who see something she doesn't. To them it's everything. To her it's just something she doesn't get. Heck, if I were her I wouldn't even have come."

"She came because of me."

"I think she'll get saved," Mike suddenly said.

I turned toward him. "Do you really think so?"

"Yeah, I do. I think she saw something here tonight that she'll never be able to get away from. I think we all did."

"Man," I whispered, "wasn't it great?"

"Yeah, until Smith came sailing in." Mike whistled softly. "I wonder what that guy's doing in the ministry. McIntyre gives out the Gospel, and Smith follows with the Boy Scout law."

"I heard that," a female voice—distinctly that of Ellie Wassom—said. "I hope you boys are not going to let the evening degenerate into a bunch of cheap gossip."

She had come quietly out of the kitchen, and Mike and I, leaning toward one another and intensely involved in our communication, hadn't heard her approach. Out in the kitchen the girls still giggled, and the rattle of ceramics against ceramics signaled an ongoing clean-up effort.

"Sorry about that," Mike told Ellie.

Ellie held a dish towel in her right hand, and she snapped it out like a whip and popped Mike on his shoulder.

"Ouch!" Mike cried.

She responded, "I know that really hurt."

"Well it did," he told her.

"Anyway," she said, "I forgive you for that nasty remark about Reverend Smith. But button your lip, boy, or I'll beat you half to death with this thing."

"Okay, Ellie," he said. "But you've got to admit that he sure put an end to what McIntyre got started.

Ellie sighed, swung the dish towel aimlessly and walked around to stand between us and the fire, effectively blocking it from our view. "Bryant Smith is what he is," she said. "He's the result of years of liberalized seminary teaching. He probably was just what you two are, back at some early point. Then he went off to seminary where he learned what you heard tonight. Just make sure you don't go off in that direction."

"At least do this for me, Ellie." I looked up at her as she loomed over us. "At least tell me which of us was right."

Shadows half hid her face, but I saw her smile. She popped the towel at me. I drew back and it missed. "You were right," she said, "but don't get the bighead over it." She became quiet, staring over us at something in the darkness. "I'm the one who has to work with Reverend Smith," she finally said, "not you. And I'm not sure how to do it. I've been fighting his kind all my life. My brother is a Nazarene preacher. I've often thought I'd be much happier with them. They're much more conservative, you know. When I left Sioux Falls, I almost made the switch. I could have gone to Nashville. Instead, I stayed in this church and came to Oklahoma City."

"I'm sure glad you did," Mike said.

"Amen," I said.

"Well, there you are," she said, coming back from a great mental distance and concentrating on us. "We're here. And there's work to be done. But I don't think we can do it by starting a war with the seminarians. Now you two get out of here and get to your cabin. Breakfast is at seven in the morning, and you guys don't look like the rise-and-shine type to me. Incidentally, I saw McIntyre out on the front porch a little while ago talking to a couple of the Putnam City boys. Who knows, we could see a couple of young men welcomed into the family before the night is over."

"Joe Ed and Dave Winchell," I said, looking to Mike.

"Let's pray for 'em," Mike said.

And we did, there in the gathering darkness of that big, cavernous room. We prayed for Connie Mason too, but she proved to be a hard fish to land.

The next morning after breakfast we started back to Oklahoma City under a beautiful blue, rain-washed sky. The storm had pushed through and was now somewhere over Fort Smith and heading east, and the whole country sparkled with the promise of new growth. I rode with Connie in her Jeep. She drove.

I saw Connie not long ago at a class reunion. She is now a grandmother, happy and contented with life from all outward appearance, and I must admit that she still looks good, having escaped the physical blows that life has dealt to some of us. I asked her if she remembered what we had gone through together in high school, and I specifically asked her about the spiritual wave that swept our school, in which so many of our classmates got saved. She assured me that she remembered it all very well, and she also said she remembered how left-out she felt, how obvious it was to her that the other kids, and I in particular, had something she just didn't have and had no idea how to get.

On the way home from Devil's Canyon, on a beautiful spring morning in 1957, with rain-cooled air washing around us in the old Jeep, I could hardly have been happier, still riding the wave of the spiritual high of the previous evening. "For some of you kids," McIntyre had said, "this night will be the most important night of your lives. For some of you, it will be just another night, and you'll forget it and go on to other things. The Savior passes by. Who will follow Him, and who will turn away?" Those words just stuck in my head, and to Connie, sitting beside me and concentrating on her driving, I must have appeared to have been dwelling on another planet.

Or did I?

I glanced over at her and saw a grim, subdued young lady unaware from all appearances of my existence. She had her hair pulled back in a ponytail, and a strand of it had come loose and was blowing around her eyes. She reached up now and then to push it back. When I spoke to her, she answered me in monosyllables. Somewhere west of El Reno she suddenly spoke in a low voice.

"We have to break up."

"What?"

"I can't be your girl anymore."

This news jolted me upright, and McIntyre's words fled away into the night from which they'd come.

"What are you talking about?" I said. "What have I done now?"

"You haven't done anything," she said. "At least I don't guess you have. You can't help what's happened. And I've tried. I've really tried to understand all this religion stuff and how it's changed you. But I don't understand it. I can't. Now you and Mike are button-holing people and telling them about Jesus, and Joe Ed says he got saved last night. Dave Winchell will follow suit pretty soon. He does everything

Joe Ed does. And Abby is right in there with you. And Charlene. And I'm left out of it all."

The last statement came out as an angry accusation, as if we had all conspired to keep her on the outside looking in.

"If you're left out," I said, "it's because you won't come in. The door's open, but you're standing on the outside by your own choice."

"No!" she snapped. "No. Don't you think I'd like to be with you on this?" She turned to me.

"Watch your driving," I said.

She jerked back to the front.

"You guys are talking about this man who was crucified two-thousand years ago as if he was sitting here in the car with us. How can you expect me to believe something like that? I don't believe it. And according to you salvation is all about believing something that I think is absurd. I never wanted any of this. We'll be seniors next year. I don't intend to spend my senior year in a nunnery. So I think it's best if we just break it off and go in different directions."

"Connie . . ." I began, but I could think of nothing to say, so I said nothing.

"I'll bring your jacket back to you on Monday," she said after we'd gone several miles in total silence.

I had been on top of the world. With a few words Connie had plunged me into the pit of despair.

We got home a little before noon. Connie dropped me at my house and sped away, leaving me on the curb bewildered and figuratively bleeding. Dad, weeding the front yard flower bed, barely looked up, and I dragged myself across the lawn and up the front steps. My brother, on the front room floor before the television set, hardly noticed my arrival, involved as he was in one of Hopalong Cassidy's adventures. Mom, ever alert, heard the front door open and close.

"That you, Doug," she called from out in the kitchen.

"Yeah," I responded.

"Have a good time?"

"Yeah."

"Want some lunch?"

"Naw. Think I'll lie down and sleep a little."

And I dragged myself back to my room and flung myself across the bed.

Ah me . . . The whole thing seems mildly amusing now, and like all aging Americans I'm inclined to dismiss it by whispering, condescendingly, "Puppy love." But if I make the effort to transport myself, mentally and emotionally, back to that time, I find that I'm not amused. I was hurting, and Connie was hurting, and neither of us knew what to do about it, other than be something we were not. I guess I could have given up my profession of Christ then and there. But Connie wouldn't have wanted me to do that. Or she could have said she'd been saved. But Connie was too honest to do that. So we stood on opposite sides of a great gulf with no way for either of us to cross over. "Just believe," I imagined myself saying to her, and I would hear her replying, "But I don't . . . I can't."

It seemed to me that I had reached an abrupt terminus of my golden youth and that nothing would ever be quite as good. Jesus had said many years ago that He had come not to bring peace, but to bring a sword, to divide families and friends. To love mother or father—or in this case Connie Mason—more than Him was to show oneself unworthy of Him. *Okay*, I thought, *it's goodbye to Connie*. I just didn't understand why it had to be this way.

I lay on my bed looking up at the ceiling, the same way I had on the night Rusty Borden was killed. Life had doubled up its fist and driven it into my solar plexus, and I was down for the count never to rise. How wrong I was! I couldn't have known it, but some of my best days were about to commence.

Later that evening a soft rain came back, whispering against the windows. Darkness crept into my room. I heard Mom and Dad talking out in the living room. Mom stuck her head into my room and said supper was ready. I said I wasn't hungry.

The telephone rang. My brother answered it.

"Doug," he yelled.

"I don't want to talk to anyone," I said.

"What in the world is the matter with you?" Mom asked.

"Nothing," I said.

"It's Connie," My brother yelled.

I bounded off the bed and into the front room like a healthy gazelle.

"Thought you didn't want to talk," I heard Mom muttering.

I seized the phone from my brother's outstretched hand.

"Connie," I said.

"I got saved," she said.

"What! How?"

"It wasn't hard at all. I was just reading in John, chapter 11, and I suddenly knew, I just knew that I believed every word of it. I know that He died for me. I would never have thought that anything like this could ever happen to me—but it did."

"Wow," I said. And again, for emphasis, "Wow!"

"Tomorrow's Sunday. Will you take me to church with you?"

"Will I ever . . . Oh, boy, I sure will!"

I don't really remember hanging up the phone. I just remember going back to my room and falling to my knees, raising my arms, fists clenched, toward the ceiling, and shouting, "Yes!"

III

BRINGING IT HOME

15

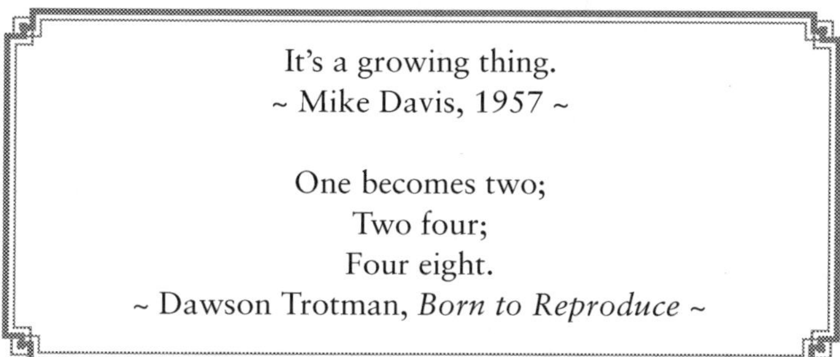

It's a growing thing.
~ Mike Davis, 1957 ~

One becomes two;
Two four;
Four eight.
~ Dawson Trotman, *Born to Reproduce* ~

I was a man on a spiritual toboggan ride, sliding along through gorgeous scenery, delighted from moment to moment as I beheld the wonders of what the Lord had done and was doing. I couldn't have started these events, and once they began I couldn't stop them. All I had to do was stay on the sled and be constantly amazed.

Before I was saved, and before the Lord had changed my life and had started dealing with me and with others, all I had known about God, as I said earlier, was religion. You went to church on Sunday, and that was where religion took place, and that was where you dealt with God and did what you ought to do about Him. The other six days of the week you rendered totally to Caesar. But a living faith operates seven days a week, twenty-four hours a day, and my feeble and meaningless religiosity, which I had always left between brick walls, beneath steeples and behind signs bearing denominational names, was about to be kicked upstairs and into a whole new dimension. I did not know this, could not have known it, but we were on our way into non-denominational home meetings. Up to this time I had never taken part in an in-depth home Bible study. There may have been such gatherings, but I surely didn't know about them. What I knew about was Sunday school in church with teachers who didn't know the Word and had only a superficial belief in what little they knew, using texts written by someone else (who also probably didn't know the Word) and filling up kids' heads with a lot of feel-good mush. No spiritual growth is possible under such teaching. All this was about to change. In fact, it had already begun to change. Kids from Classen High School were getting together in homes for prayer meetings, and Ellie Wassom was meeting with them, and teenagers who had never given the Lord Jesus Christ a serious thought were learning that He is a real, living Savior.

Think back to the Devil's Canyon retreat and to my sad encounter with the preacher who had no use for blood atonement. Ellie Wassom was there to witness that, as were Mike Davis, Bill Sam Knight, Nancy McNatt and the church kids, Connie Mason, some of the Putnam City crowd, and a new arrival, Alan Trimble. And there were two others I haven't mentioned up to now—Bob and Evon Potter. How I have come this far without saying anything about them seems odd as I look back over what I have written. Perhaps I have saved the best for the last.

Bob was a good-looking man. Evon was beyond good-looking. I have always thought she could have doubled for the young Jennifer Jones. They were perhaps ten or twelve years older than any of us high schoolers. Bob had married Evon while they were still in Capitol Hill High School, then had promptly gone off to Japan to get in on the last few months of the War and to serve in the occupational army. He came home and went into the supermarket business, and he and Evon got busy setting up a household and producing three sons. They were well-off, fast-living and fairly miserable without realizing it. They ran with the cocktail crowd, went to semi-sophisticated parties, dressed well, drove nice cars and spent money going nowhere fast. They were living the American dream that all G.I.s fantasized about while they were down in foxholes dodging death. The dream was a fatuous nightmare. But the Lord had plans for them that did not include cornering the market on a glittering garbage heap. Bob and Evon became my spiritual parents. First, however, the Lord had to save them.

I knew them because they went to church where I did. Our church, as I have already explained, was carefully constructed to offend as few as possible, a religious club for those on their way up and out.

Then, in the summer of 1956, Billy Graham came to town, and lives started getting rearranged. Mike Davis got saved. Several Sunday School teachers got saved. Bob Potter got saved.

Evon got upset.

What was she to make of this nonsense? Her good-looking, social-climbing husband had begun toting a Bible and talking about Jesus. One afternoon while Bob was at work, her two older sons were in school and her baby was down for a nap, Evon began talking to God in a way that she never had before. She got her Bible down from the top shelf of a bookcase, blew off the dust (her words, not mine) and said, "God, if this guy Graham is telling the truth, I want to know it." Then she closed her eyes, opened the Bible, put her finger down on a page, opened her eyes and looked. She was pointing to Malachi 3:1: *Behold, I will send my messenger, and he shall prepare the way before Me; and the Lord, whom ye seek, shall suddenly come to His temple.* Now Evon said many times, looking back at this incident, that this is not the way she determined the Lord's will for her life after she was saved and had come to a measure of spiritual maturity; but she also said that she was very certain the Lord, ever and always gracious, had guided her hand on this occasion and had spoken to her in answer to her simple prayer. That night at Billy's meeting she got saved.

Bob and Evon had been saved less than a year the night of the Devil's Canyon incident. They were hanging around with the young people, going out to the Classen meetings some, trying to help Ellie out, trying to do what good they could but with very little to offer. They were themselves spiritual babes. Still, even in their immaturity they knew the preacher was wrong, and that I (ignorant though I may have been) was right because I had the clear backing of the Word of God. So after the retreat Bob went in to see the preacher and tell him that he and Evon were leaving the church.

"No need to be hasty," the preacher said. "We can work this out."

"There's nothing to work out," Bob told him. "What you're doing and what we're doing are two different things."

And out the door he went and never looked back.

But what to do now? They knew they had to be in fellowship with other believers, and they knew there was no place for them in the church they had just left. They just didn't know where they ought to go.

But God knew.

Bob's grocery store was located on Northeast 23rd Street in Oklahoma City, about a mile east of the state capitol building. About two blocks farther east stood a church with a sign out front which read, "Is it nothing to you, all ye that pass by?" And it probably *was* very little or nothing to most of those rushing up and down this busy thoroughfare, but it became something of great importance to Bob and Evon Potter. Bob's mother introduced him to the pastor, a Dallas Theological Seminary graduate named David Cotten, and the two became fast and life-long friends. Bob and Evon began meeting with the Christians at Metropolitan Baptist Church. Pastor Cotten was another Jim McIntyre, another Ellie Wassom, another of those true believers who did not take the clear Word of God and allegorize it into meaninglessness.

Meanwhile, back in the hallowed halls of Putnam City High School, I was wandering around making myself obnoxious to the student population. And yet there was a small but growing group of kids, including some of the jocks, who had thrown in with me and were willing to declare their faith in Jesus Christ openly and without fear or shame. Connie Mason had actually begun to try to share the Lord with some of the other cheerleaders. All of us had an obvious and crippling problem—we were as dumb as logs. We had Bibles, but we knew very little about what was in them.

We were in an interesting predicament, now that I think about it. The organized churches we attended on Sundays couldn't help us because we had no actual connection to any of them. We were seeing kids saved in the halls of high school, in the streets, in malt shops, out on the fringes and apart from any recognized religious institutions. We didn't plan it this way. It just happened. If the Baptists had started some sort of meetings for us, the Methodists probably would not have felt welcome. If the Methodists had got the meetings up, the Baptists would probably not have attended. So we did nothing, other than what we had been doing. We went to Young Life meetings, and we went to church, and we tried to read our Bibles, and we tried to pray, and beyond these rather obvious activities we just simply hung out and gave out the Gospel in a feeble, amateur fashion.

Classen High School's home meetings might have served as an example for us, but we knew of no one in Putnam City who could take the lead. Ellie Wassom had her hands full with church and with what was going on at Classen. Jim McIntyre would probably have been willing to take up the challenge, but he worked at a full time job supporting his family. The Young Life leaders were busy with the clubs at Putnam City and Capitol Hill and were looking at branching out into Harding and Northwest Classen. Beyond these we knew of no adults who knew any more about the Bible than we did, and we knew of absolutely none who had evidenced any deep commitment to the Lord. And, frankly, we were typical of so many teens—we just didn't trust adults very much. We didn't think they understood us. So we envied the Classen crowd, and we waited.

16

> And the things that thou hast heard of me among many witnesses, the same commit thou to faithful men who shall be able teach others also.
> ~ Paul to Timothy (II Tim. 2:2) ~
>
> Other fell into good ground, and brought forth fruit.
> ~ Jesus (Matt. 13:8) ~

One fine evening in the early spring of 1957, Bob and Evon came home from some activity to find a strange car parked in their driveway, and leaning against it, arms crossed, was a young man neither of them had ever laid eyes on. Now Bob was not the paranoid type, but his first thought was that a strange car plus a strange man could equal bad news.

"You know him?" he asked Evon.

"Nope," she said. "I thought you did."

The three kids in the back seat said nothing, except for the one in the middle who was being teased by his older brother.

"You two quiet down," Bob said.

"He's poking me with his finger," said the one being tormented.

The man on the driveway had left his position against the car and had started toward the Potters. He was a small, young fellow with wavy black hair and dark eyes, dressed in khakis, a knit golf shirt, and brown loafers. He was smiling. He waved. Bob waved back and leaned out the driver's side window.

"What's up?" Bob asked.

"Potter?"

"Yeah."

"Jack Holt," the young man said, extending his hand as he came within arm's reach.

Bob shook his hand.

"He's making a face at me," one of the kids in the back seat said.

"Be quiet," said Evon.

"This is the third time I've been by to see you," the man told Bob. "I was about to give up."

"If he's an insurance salesman," Evon whispered to Bob, "we don't need any."

"I'm with the Navigators," said the young man.

Bob said nothing because he had no idea what to say. He had never heard of the Navigators.

"You've never heard of us, have you?"

Bob shook his head.

"Most folks haven't. Well, how about Billy Graham. Have you ever heard of him?

"Well, sure . . ."

"Let's just say that Billy sent me."

By this time the Potters were out of their car and gathering around the young stranger.

"Sent you to do what?" Bob asked.

"To follow up on what began when you went forward in his meetings. To get you growing in your Christian life."

"Well, okay, but . . ."

"Oh, Bob," Evon said, "let's not stand around on the driveway. Come on in, Mr. Holt."

"Jack."

"Come on in, Jack," Bob said.

It was a simple enough meeting, with the usual pleasantries exchanged, but it was a meeting fraught with spiritual potential beyond anything that any of those on the driveway that evening could have imagined.

Bob and Evon had only recently had a room built on to the back of their suburban home, and it was here that they sat down around a table with coffee and began to get to know the visitor. Because of the room's importance to many of us, I'll have a go at describing it. The home itself was situated west of Portland on 18th Street, just south of Saint Patrick's Catholic Church. If you entered the home through the front door, you found yourself in a typical living room. You passed out of the living room through the dining room and, as the home was originally designed, ran smack up against the house's back wall. The Potters, however, had knocked out a chunk of the wall and put in a double door, so that instead of having your progress arrested by brick and mortar you stepped down into a room that was almost as big as the rest of house. The floor was tile of some species. To the right in the room's northwest corner was a sink, a built-in range with oven, cabinets around a large window, a table and some chairs. A refrigerator was also over there somewhere, but I have forgotten exactly how it fit in.

On the left stood floor-to-ceiling bookcases. Chairs of different sorts were scattered about. Covering the floor, more or less in the center, was a large round rug, not Persian, but not cheap. Directly ahead, so that to reach the south wall you had to go around it, was a large couch. It could be made into a bed if circumstances demanded. On the wall in front of the couch was a wood burning fireplace. On the wall, over the fireplace, hung a picture of Jesus. And to the fireplace's right, as you stood facing it, was a piano. Why they had a piano I do not know—neither Bob nor Evon played so far as I remember. But that piano served a very useful purpose once the meetings got going.

Rarely did anyone enter the Potter home through the front door. I don't ever recall going in that way, and I was in their home many times. We always came in through the door on the home's west side, which led from the driveway directly into the large add-on room, which we called the den. It was through this door that the Potters and their guest entered on that late summer evening.

They sat around the table in the kitchen corner.

"I'll put on some coffee," Evon said.

"Great," said Jack.

"All right, Mr. Navigator," Bob said, "start navigating. Who in the world are the Navigators, anyway?"

It was a long story. Jack didn't leave until after ten o'clock.

Dawson Trotman, the founder of the Navigators, was saved when he was a young man in California. "The man was a genius," Bob Potter used to say. Maybe he was, and maybe not, but he was certainly an innovator, and he was a leader, and he was a natural—born motivator. He became convinced early in his Christian experience that victorious Christian living required something more than a pat on the back, a "God bless you, son," and a "Go to church next Sunday." What was needed, more specifically, was four something mores: the Bible, prayer, fellowship, and witnessing to others about Jesus Christ. Unlike Billy Graham, who conducted meetings before large audiences, Daws gave his life to working in small groups, and often with only one man at a time. He theorized that if one became two, and two four, then by a geometric progression the whole world could be reached for Christ in one man's life time. This was what the Navigator's were all about.

But how did this get Jack Holt into the Potter home?

Early in his career Billy Graham had become concerned about the lack of follow-up ministry for those who came forward in his meetings. As far back as reliable history took him, he saw no evangelists making any efforts to follow up their converts. In fact, the very idea seemed a bit impossible. With thousands coming forward during a crusade, how could a follow-up work be put together? Graham contacted his old friend Daws Trotman.

"Billy," said Daws, "I'm not getting done what the Lord has given me to do as it is. I can't take six months away from my work to spend with you. You'll have to get someone else."

According to Daws, Billy took him by the shoulders, shook him a bit and said, "Who? Who else is majoring in this sort of thing?"

Graham must have been imminently persuasive because Daws became a part of the team. In fact, Daws and his Navigators created the first effective follow-up ministry to be attached to any of history's Gospel crusades, barring perhaps the crusades of the Apostle Paul. They worked like this. If an individual went forward at one of Billy's meetings, he was ushered aside to an area set up for the occasion, and he was asked to fill out a card with his name, address, telephone number and denominational preference. These cards were then handed over to the Navigators, who sent one of their people to contact the new convert and get him into an in-home training program.

The Navigators were always big on Scripture memory and topical Bible studies. The memorizing of Scripture got the Word out of a leather-bound, dust-covered book and into heart and mind, ready and available to be used as needed. If I am tempted, I access Corinthians 10:13; if I sin and want God's forgiveness, I rely on I John 1:9. The topical Bible studies took the babe in Christ to God's Word in a practical way, introducing him or her not only to important doctrines, but also to biblical teaching about how one ought to conduct his or her life. There was also a good deal of group prayer in all the Navigator sessions.

Jack explained all this to Bob and Evon that evening as they sat around the table in the den, sipping coffee and getting acquainted. They agreed to meet on Saturday evenings, every Saturday, for as long as it took to get the Potters on their spiritual feet and going down the road. Jack gave each of them a packet of Bible verses and simply said, "Memorize them."

"By when?" Evon asked.

"By next Saturday."

"I've got a rotten memory," Bob said.

Evon said, "Mine's worse."

"Memorize them," Jack said.

"Pushy character," Bob told Evon after Jack had left.

"I like him," said Evon. "I think he's just what we need—because, let's face it, neither of us have the vaguest idea what we're doing."

"Makes you wonder what we were doing in church all those years."

The following Saturday evening at seven o'clock Jack showed up. Neither Bob nor Evon had memorized all the verses.

"There were only ten verses," Jack said. "Oh, well. Here are ten more."

"Pushy," Bob later told Evon.

But they both persevered. By the fourth Saturday both Bob and Evon had memorized over thirty Bible verses, were working on a fourth pack of ten, were both spending time alone with God and His Word early every morning, were keeping prayer journals and prayer lists and were deep into a study of growth in the Christian life.

"Look at Second Timothy," Jack told them, "chapter two, verse two."

They were at the table in the den, Bibles open, notebooks open, pens poised above paper. A few weeks ago both would have had to struggle to find the reference. In fact, both had felt like fools compared to Jack, and both were slightly ashamed to admit that they had grown up in church and knew so little about this Book that they had always claimed to believe. But they were getting better, more familiar with the various books and where to find them.

"*The things that thou hast heard of me among many witnesses, the same commit thou to faithful men, who shall be able to teach others also.*" Jack paused, sipped coffee and went on. "The key word here is faithful. Notice what we have here. Paul taught Timothy. But he didn't teach him so that he could simply have knowledge. Timothy was supposed to pass it on. But pass it on to who?"

Evon wanted to say, "To whom," but she actually said, "To faithful men."

"Why faithful men?"

"Why waste your time on someone who won't do anything with what you give them?" Bob said.

Jack laughed. "Okay," he said. "I guess that about gets to the heart of it. There's a multiplication principle at work here. Daws Trotman used to say that anyone he ever knew who accomplished anything for the Lord . . . it wasn't because they were smart or talented. It was because they were faithful. Because they could be counted on. I hate to be the one to tell you this, but most of the folks I run into in this business can't be counted on for much of anything. I hope you two are different."

"We'll find out soon enough," Bob told him.

Jack smiled and nodded.

Three people with Bibles—one a grocer, one a housewife, one a college student, none an ordained minister or even a theologian—sounds counter-intuitive, when you think about it. But those three became four, and those four became eight, and the study lasted for over two years, and individuals who came to the Potters' home on Saturday evenings in the late 1950s are today all over the world in full-time Christian work.

On a warm Saturday evening in the summer of 1957, Jack, Bob and Evon were discussing Second Timothy, verse two, and Jack had taken them to Acts 18 to show them how spiritual multiplication works in practice. What happened next remains to me one of the great unknowns of the whole deal. Many years after the fact Bob Potter and I sat over lunch discussing how the Bible study in his home got started, and he told me the story just as I relate it here.

The back door opened, and there, unannounced, stood Mike Davis. The mystery is why he was there at all. He knew Bob and Evon from church, but I don't believe that any of the kids from my age group, including Mike, knew them well. They were from the older crowd. As I have already mentioned, after Bob and Evon had been saved they began doing what they could to help Ellie Wassom in the church youth group. Maybe they had hooked up with Mike at one of the Sunday evening get-togethers. Maybe they came out to some of the Classen meetings. Maybe one of them had invited Mike to come over. Maybe . . . I could fill in the blank space with a hundred "maybes" and still get it wrong. The simple truth is that Mike showed up because God directed him to the Potters' home that evening. The rest, as they say, is history.

Did Mike have a Bible with him? Don't be silly. Kids that age, even those who had gone forward in Billy's meetings, rarely carried Bibles around. Mike sat at the table and listened as Jack opened up Acts 18.

Paul had left Athens and gone to Corinth, and there he had been taken in by a Christian couple (Jews, as was Paul) named Priscilla and Aquilla. Paul and Aquilla had a common trade: both were tent makers.

"Imagine having Paul living with you for a month or so, maybe even a year." Jack paused to give the others time to think about that. "Would that be a learning experience, or what?"

"He'd probably get under foot," Evon said.

"I've got a crazy guy named Paul in my history class," Mike announced. "He's under foot and under intelligent, and he's probably under indictment." This was not helpful, but it succeeded in getting a laugh.

"You've got a future on the stage," Jack told him.

"Yeah," Mike said. "I know the punch line to that one. On the stage—either Wells Fargo or Western Overland."

"All right, back to the Book."

Jack took them down to the end of the chapter and showed them that Paul had gone to Ephesus, taking Priscilla and Aquilla with him. In the Ephesian synagogue one day Priscilla and Aquilla heard a young man named Apollos debating, and they were mightily impressed, for he was eloquent, learned in the Scriptures and fervent. But he was also ignorant, knowing only the baptism of John the Baptist. So they took him home with them and taught him the truth of the Lord Jesus Christ more perfectly.

"Now, notice the progression here," Jack said. "Paul teaches Priscilla and Aquilla and they pass on what they have learned to Apollos, and he goes out and becomes one of the most powerful teachers in the first century church."

He turned to Mike. "What's your name, funny man?"

"Mike."

"Okay, suppose Mike is Apollos, and suppose Bob and Evon are Priscilla and Aquilla. That makes me Paul. I teach you two, you pass on what you've learned to Mike, and Mike goes out and rocks the civilized world. Stranger things have happened. Feel like rocking the world, buddy?" Jack leaned across the table and gripped Mike's hand. "Don't think God can't use you. All He needs is a faithful man."

They talked on, late into the night, until Evon reminded them that they all had to get up and go to church in the morning.

Mike leaned back in his chair, drove his right fist into his open left hand and said, "Boy! This is the greatest night I've had since I went forward at Billy's meeting. Can I come back?"

It was an odd request, coming from one who had come in uninvited and unannounced to begin with. It didn't matter, however, because they were all delighted to have him.

"What if I bring some of the other kids?" he said. "I'd like to bring Doug Miller, and maybe Trimble. Maybe Nancy McNatt."

"Sure," Bob said. "Bring them along."

"Hold on," Jack said. "There are some rules that go with this business. First, we start at seven on the dot. You don't wander in late. You bring a Bible with you, and you read Second Timothy. And here . . ." He fished into a briefcase he had placed on the floor beside his chair and drew out a small packet. "Memorize these ten verses and quote them back to me next Saturday. That's your entrance ticket."

He slid the packet across the table to Mike, who took it up, looked on one side, turned it over, looked at the other, and said, "I can't memorize these."

Jack twisted his lips into the facsimile of a grin. "Where have I heard that?" he asked.

"I cannot memorize these verses," Mike insisted.

"I'll bet you can," Jack told him. "I know very well that you can. And if you don't, keep trying until you do. And when you do, then you'll be welcome to come to this humble meeting. And if you think I'm being cruel, just remember what Jesus said to the rich young ruler."

"What was that?"

"Read the story in Matthew 19. I'll be kinder to you than the Lord Jesus would have been. He was a Man on his way to the cross to die for bums like you and me. Memorize these verses, Mike."

"Pushy fellow," Mike told me at church on Sunday morning, when he was filling me in on last evening's events.

"Well, have you memorized the verses?"

"I'm working on 'em, Miller. But listen, buddy, you need to come over to the Potters' place next Saturday. You'll hear things you've never heard before. We're into something better than anything we ever got into in our lives."

He showed me the packet of ten verses Jack Holt had given him, and I wrote the references down. In the following week I memorized all ten verses just to get a leg up on Jack Holt, and just because I was a little too smart for my own good, and just because the Spirit of God was working in me to conform me to the image of Jesus Christ my Lord. Those verses laid the foundation for my life as a believer. They were the first ten of what became several hundred. Since that day I have told many believers that they ought to be memorizing Scripture, only to have them reply that they can't because they have poor memories.

"I'll bet you can," I always say, "if you really want to."

And they probably went away and said to the first person they met, "Pushy fellow, that Miller."

17

> Before we knew it, there were fifty
> And sixty showing up.
> ~ Bob Potter ~
>
> Avalanche: a sudden great or overwhelming rush of something.
> ~ *Webster's Collegiate Dictionary* ~

We started meeting at Bob and Evon Potter's home on Saturday evenings, and the whole thing just snowballed. College kids started coming in from Stillwater, along with high school kids from Classen and Capitol Hill and Putnam City. There were Baptists and Methodists and Presbyterians and strange individuals from the other side of the denominational tracks who spoke in tongues and jumped over benches. Some of the sailors from the air station in Norman started showing up. I have no idea how they heard of the meeting if not by word of mouth, because there was never an attempt made to do any sort of formal advertising via newspaper or radio.

I found out something that year that I have never forgotten—that denominations are as meaningless to a true believer as opera music is to a down-home country singer. My particular church was filled with people tagged with a denominational name, whose names appeared on the church rolls, who showed up Sunday after Sunday to go through the religious motions, and with whom I had nothing in common spiritually. In Bob's and Evon's home I found myself surrounded by individuals to whom I was drawn because they were saved, and they loved the Lord, and they were indwelt by the same Holy Spirit Who had taken up residency in me. We didn't argue methods of baptism, nor eschatological positions, nor any of the things that usually divide believers; we just enjoyed one another's company and learned from one another. This was over fifty years ago. To this day I do not like denominationalism. I learned something about the unity of the Body of Christ that summer at Potter's place, and I have become a sworn enemy of anything or anyone who divides the community of faith by saying, "I am of Paul," or, "I am of Apollos."

Saturday night in the Potter home became the most important thing going on for many of us in Oklahoma City in 1957 and 1958. It seems strange now, looking back at it. Saturday night should have been the time to pile into cars and drag Main Street, or dance to jukebox music at the soda shop, or spend necking with your girl on the back row of the local theater without ever bothering to see what unfolded on the big screen. But to tuck a Bible under your arm and head off to meet with a group of Christians and discuss the Lord . . . well, who could have imagined it?

Some might ask exactly what we did between the hours of seven and nine on any given Saturday. It's been many years ago, but as I remember it we always began by singing. Someone who could play the piano teamed up with someone who could wave his arms in an appropriate fashion, and someone passed out songbooks that Bob or Evon had gotten from somewhere, and we sang. Then Jack Holt would generally stand up and ask if anyone had anything they would like to share. Generally, those who shared would tell of answered prayers, or of something particularly meaningful to them that they had read in the Bible during a quiet time, or of how the Lord had helped them through a difficult time. Then we would split up into smaller groups, each led by someone who had been down the road with the Lord far enough to qualify as something other than an absolute novice. The discussions rarely covered anything doctrinal, though we did talk about salvation by grace through faith and about believing the gospel. We talked about dispensations too, and I heard for the first time about the pre-tribulational rapturing of the Church. Many of the attendees carried Scofield Bibles. But for the most part our discussions centered in on very practical matters, life as we experienced it day to day, what a Christian ought to be doing and saying, how we ought to conduct ourselves. Encouraged by the

Navigators or their associates, almost all of us were memorizing Bible verses, and we spent a certain amount of time reviewing these.

In chapter 4 of *The Great Gatsby* Nick Carraway lists the people he could remember who came to parties at Gatsby's home one summer. It is a brilliant piece of writing, one that I could not hope to imitate in my wildest fantasies; nevertheless allow me, Fitzgerald-like, to rummage about in the cavity of my aging mind and reconstruct, as best I am able, a roster of those who showed up at the Potters', Bibles in hand, to drink collectively from the Fountain of Living Waters.

From Classen High School came Mike Davis, as natural and unspoiled a comedian as one could ever have hoped to meet. And Alan Trimble came along toting his Scofield Bible with the seal skin cover. Fred Suhre came with his sweetheart Nancy Medley. Nancy McNatt was there, togged out in jeans, two-toned saddle oxfords and her father's cast-off white shirts, tail out and sleeves rolled up. Angie Olson usually came with Nancy, and they brought with them a blind girl, Keddy Kaye Jones, who carried this enormous Braille Bible and simply radiated joy. Billy Reynolds came some of the time, and Rob Horner came when the Saturday evening television schedule was sufficiently boring. He brought Pattie Wheat with him once, but she got into an argument with Mike Davis over something so frivolous I can't even remember it (and I doubt she or Mike do), and she never came back.

Jack Holt was always there, of course. I probably should explain that Jack was not on staff with the Navigators. Lots of those working with the Navs were volunteers, just like Jack. He was working on a degree in agriculture from OSU, but he was self-employed as a carpenter. A bunch of the OSU students who knew Jack came to the meetings with him. Bob Doty, a student manager for the football team, came, and Joe Lee Holt (no relation to Jack), the team's right tackle, and an education major named Melba, whose last name I have forgotten and with whom all the boys were at least slightly in love.

From the naval air base in Norman Rich Boyer came when he could get off duty. Sometimes he wore his uniform and sometimes he did not. He was unlike any sailor I had ever met or ever even imagined; he neither drank, nor swore, nor hung around with loose women of questionable habits. And a nurse came. I don't remember her name. She too had a military connection of some sort, Air Force I believe, stationed at Tinker as I recall.

From Putnam City I came, and Connie Mason came with me. Kenny McClain came and usually brought several with him. Bill Sam Knight never missed a Saturday night. Joe Ed Tracy and Dave Winchell came when Dave could get his car running. Abby French came along with Lou Ann Sanders, whenever one of them could come up with a car. Abby could have come with Joe Ed if Lou Ann hadn't insisted on tagging along. For reasons I can only guess at, Joe Ed and Lou Ann never quite hit it off. Joe Hanks had a weekend job parking cars at this high-class restaurant, and we rarely saw him. Jim McIntyre and his wife Mary came some of the time, if they could get a babysitter for their kids. Ellie came only once, as I remember, because (Who but God knows why?) she didn't care for the format.

One man who came with his wife had been an admitted homosexual. I doubt that many of those in the study knew of this man's struggles, or his victories and his defeats. I know because he told me. He never asked me to keep this to myself, but I did until now. I have no idea what ever became of him.

And there were others, many others, who passed through the open door of Bob and Evon Potter's home and went back out into the world. Some hovered around the fringes like the mixed multitude that followed Moses out of Egypt. Some came to scoff and remained to pray. Some never amounted to a hill of beans for the Lord. Some served, and some are still serving. None who saw what happened at that time can doubt that this was indeed a mighty moving of the Holy Spirit among individuals who seemed, by any consideration, the least likely to be moved.

18

> That was a long time ago, Nell.
> ~ Johnny Shawnesy in *Raintree County* ~
>
> A long life may not be good enough,
> But a good life is long enough.
> ~ A note Bill Sam Knight wrote in his Bible ~

That fall, my senior year, the football team came into its own. We simply murdered our opponents. I was a co-captain, along with Troy Freeman, and I played left end, from which position I caught five touchdown passes. For a good part of the season we were ranked number one in the state. Now I sit here, fifty years and more into the future and looking back, and I can't quite remember what life was like. I remember that the nights were cool and dusted with stars, that the field onto which we ran was green and marked with chalk lines, that people jammed the stands and stood up to cheer, that flash bulbs from a dozen cameras seemed to go off like silent bombs and sprayed dazzling light onto the field, that the band played our fight song, that the cheerleaders could hardly be heard above the roaring crowd, and that the girls in the pep club stood up and sang, "Oh when those Putnam Pirates fall in line, we're gonna win that game another time . . ."

It's all gone. Did I really think it would last forever?

Not long ago I walked the halls of Putnam City High School, stopped at the trophy case outside the gymnasium, looked at the mosaic pirate's head on the floor, and watched the students hustling by on their way to classes. Not one of them stopped, awe-stricken, to look at me. Not one of them called to friends, "Look, it's Doug

Miller." Not one of them had the vaguest idea who Doug Miller is. The paths of glory indeed lead but to the grave. The paths of righteousness, as God fosters it in those of faith . . . ah, that's another matter.

At some point that fall several of us started meeting in the mornings before classes to pray together and read the Bible. Putnam City Baptist Church was directly across the street from the high school, on Fortieth and Grove, and several of my friends went to church there. Kenny McClain, whose father taught Sunday school, approached the pastor, Max Stanfield, and asked if we could use the church in the mornings. He had no objections and said he'd leave the door open for us. The door he left open was the door to the basement, a large room with good lighting and folding chairs set up in a sort of semi-circular arrangement around a podium. There were never more than ten or twelve of us, but we met Monday through Friday, at seven o'clock, and we prayed, and I would usually read the Scripture and give a brief message. I can't remember at this late date, nor can I imagine, what I talked about, or why anyone would have come out early in the morning to listen. Of course, most did not. But some did. And it is from this humble get-together that the home prayer meeting began.

A prayer meeting? Among a bunch of high school kids? A meeting unattached to any sort of organization or church? Are you kidding me?

The very idea seems strange at best and downright silly at worst. Who could be expected to come? Well, those who came out to the morning meetings at the church might show up, and some of those who were going to Bob and Evon Potter's home on the weekends would probably wander in from time to time. But when and where would we hold the meetings? Bill Sam Knight, Kenny McClain and I were the main ones kicking the idea around, and we could think of a dozen reasons why it would never work and not one good reason why it would. Bill Sam had graduated from high school in 1957 and had matriculated at Oklahoma Baptist University for the fall semester, but he had no problem making himself available for the meetings unless they conflicted with his schedule. In fact, they conflicted with everyone's schedule. We could not hold meetings on Saturday night because we wanted to go to Potter's meeting. We could not hold them on Sunday or Wednesday evenings because that would put us in unwanted competition with the churches. Young Life met on Monday nights. Friday was absolutely out because Friday night was our night to drag Main Street, go to movies, to boogie and in general make ourselves obnoxious to adults and guardians of the establishment. Besides, we played football on Friday nights. This took us down to Thursday and Tuesday.

Time has past and my memory has gone west with the setting sun. I believe we met on Tuesday nights, but it may have been Thursday.

And what were we to call this get-together? We might have given it a fancy name if we had been clever enough to think of one. We might have called ourselves the Jesus Club, but that seemed a bit outrageous, perhaps even blasphemous. We toyed with SOW (servants of the Word), but that never stuck. Various theological, cosmological and sociological titles made the rounds among the handful of us who seriously believed we ought to summon such a strange assembly. No name we thought of really worked. Finally, we just called it the prayer meeting, without bothering even to capitalize the first letters.

If any out there doubt that the Lord in His mysterious wisdom moved us to start the prayer meeting, let that doubter ask himself or herself what better explanation the facts of the business call forth. God must have been at work, otherwise something so ostensibly stupid would never have gotten off the ground, or never gotten to first base, or never . . . whatever hackneyed phrase one cares to use in place of the ones I just used.

We first met at Connie Mason's home on a Tuesday evening. Mr. and Mrs. Mason loved me like a son, and they loved Connie like a true daughter—which she was—but they had no idea what we were up to. When Connie told them some of the kids were coming over to pray, which she casually mentioned to them that very morning at breakfast, they looked at her as if she had just announced she intended to spray-paint dirty words on the governor's mansion. The Masons had hosted parties of various sorts over the years. They had even had Young Life meetings in their home. But this took the proverbial cake.

"Going to what?" Mrs. Mason asked.

"To pray," Connie said, with feigned naïve innocence that only she could muster.

"I suppose the Right Reverend Miller has his hand in this enterprise," Mr. Mason said. He really did like me. He just didn't understand me.

"He'll be here," Connie said, buttering her toast and smiling.

Of course the Masons let us use their den. Assuming they possessed the gentility one expects in upper-middle class suburban parents—and they certainly did, and then some—they could hardly have turned her down. Dance to Elvis Presley in the den, sure. Pray together . . . not in my home. It just wouldn't have worked. So at seven o'clock about ten of us sat down in a room that would have done Ozzie and Harriet Nelson proud while Mr. and Mrs. Mason retreated to the relative sanctuary of the den, and we held a prayer meeting in the living room. Present were two cheerleaders, three football players and an individual destined to translate the New Testament out of Greek and into simple English for use in inland China. Bill Sam was there too. He and the translator-to-be were a little on the nerdish side. As for the rest, we were big fish in a very small pond.

The meeting's format never changed much over time. I followed what I'd seen done at Bob's and Evon's and what we had been doing in the basement of the Baptist church. We read from the Bible, asked if anybody wanted to share anything and then started praying. What did we pray for, and who prayed? I don't remember what or who. I remember, however, that usually Bill Sam or McClain would be designated to begin the praying, and I would deliver the closer, and in between anyone who wanted to could pray.

The meeting was migratory. The next week we gathered at Abby French's home, then at Joe Ed's, then wherever we could find kindly souls who would take us in. We were never disorderly or noisy, never wrecked anything or tore up any furniture, and no one ever came in drunk or even tipsy. We came to pray.

It sounds loose, unsupervised, potentially chaotic, potentially schismatic, potentially heretical, potentially troubling to all those accustomed to business as usual in many churches. It is a wonder that the more conventional among the adults did not rise up en masse and shut us down. Actually, they tried in as non-offensive a way as they could; they tried by asking questions, of us and of one another. Who were the leaders? What organization sponsored us? Why were no adults involved? What doctrine did we espouse concerning water baptism? Concerning predestination? Concerning the notion of falling from grace as opposed to the eternal security of the believer? What did Reverend So-and-So think of our activities? The answers they got could have done nothing but raise more questions and stir up more trepidation. There were no adults, no sponsors, no churches guiding. And who, by the way, was the Reverend So-and-So?

We were driving our parents crazy. They were supposed to be helping us through the typical adolescent problems of acne, puppy love and juvenile delinquency, not trying to figure out why we insisted on getting together to pray. Why, they probably wondered, didn't we go out and steal hubcaps like other self-respecting teens?

"Hell if I know," Abby French quoted her father as saying. Then he quickly smiled, according to Abby, and said, "Oops . . . pardon my French. That Miller kid came over to the house one night," he went on, "talking like a holy roller. I kind of like the kid, though. I just can't figure out what makes him tick."

None of the parents seemed to be able to figure out what was making their sons and daughters tick, and none, including those of us who started the meetings, could really figure out why people started coming out. There were ten. Then there were twenty. And within a matter of months upwards of fifty and sixty high school students were coming out on Tuesday nights to pray together.

Few of those parents are alive today, and those who are may well have forgotten the anxiety and the bewilderment a bunch of praying kids caused them. I know Mr. and Mrs. French are both dead. I went to Mr. Mason's funeral not long ago. He had outlived his wife. But if any remain and are listening, I would like to tell you exactly what drove and motivated your praying children at Putnam City High School in the fall of 1957 and the spring of 1958. I could have told you then if you would have listened.

We had been raised in Sunday schools and churches. We uniformly thought of ourselves as Christian. We knew about God, knew some things about Jesus, said we believed the Bible, said we believed in eternal life, paid lip service to the ideas of heaven and hell. We all knew how to pray the Lord's Prayer, and some of us even knew the Apostles' Creed by heart. That was about as far as it went with any of us. Then Rusty Borden died, and I got saved. The other kids heard about this, didn't know what to make of it and began to watch me to see if I would morph into a dark, tortured creature from a Hawthorne novel. I imagine they thought that my religious oddness wouldn't last long, and that in short order I would reclaim my sanity and return to a more normal and non-offensive posture. As time went on and I seemed determined to go on with the Lord, others came out of hiding and began to openly admit their agreement with me. And of course my position as captain of the football team did no harm to the cause.

But all of this is purely secular with a little pseudo-psychology thrown in. The real reason the kids flocked out to the prayer meeting was because the Holy Spirit had begun to move like a mighty wind through the entire city, possibly as a result of the Graham meetings, certainly as a result of the prayers of people like Jim McIntyre and Ellie Wassom. The Holy Spirit's business is to glorify the Son of God. He did just this, up and down the hallowed halls of Putnam City High School, and in Classen and Capitol Hill, and even in Cassidy. Jesus Christ shone forth in beauty and glory, dying and raised up from the dead, alive for evermore and drawing troubled, confused teenagers to Himself.

"Come out to our prayer meeting tonight," I said.

"What are you gonna do?"

"Pray."

There is not one credible reason why anyone should have responded to this invitation, even if the football captain issued it. But they did, in fact, respond. Accept the truth, or reject it—they came for a supernatural reason. This was the hand of the Lord.

It goes without saying, but I'll say it anyway. The impact of these meetings on the school and the student body was just simply tremendous. Even some of the teachers were touched by what they saw in the students. An air of spiritual dynamism vibrated in the school, unseen but very real, very tangible. People coming in off the streets who had nothing to do with the student body or the educational process—salesmen, parents, policemen—could feel, in ways none could explain, that this place was different. And occasionally someone would ask, and we had a chance to tell them. Some listened. Some did not. Some had their lives changed while some went their way and never knew that they had been close to eternal life. I suppose that's the way it works.

19

Let him that thinketh he standeth
take heed lest he fall.
~ I Cor. 10:12 ~

Draw me nearer, nearer, blessed Lord
To Thy precious, bleeding side.
~ Fannie Crosby ~

We come to the end, and I find that I must talk about myself. Not that I mind talking about myself. In fact I would be less than honest if I did not admit that I am one of my favorite subjects. Most of my friends would not hesitate to put an "amen" to that statement. But it is not always a pleasant exercise when one is forced, as I now am, to admit to gross and painful failure. I suppose I could just as easily skip this part and pretend that I went from victory to victory, but that would not only be a lie, it would not be helpful. Through my failure I learned some lessons that I wish, in closing, to pass on for the particular benefit of young people and for the benefit of any who have been saved, who went on well, or who slipped and fell and have never been able to get back up.

Listen to me! God is not through with you.

I have written this account from my personal perspective because I don't know how else it might have been written; and thus it is, in the strictest of senses, my story. Any number of others who lived through this with me might tell the story differently, from their perspective, and then it would be their story. However, in view of the position I occupied near the center as these events unfolded, I believe I should tell it. That means, however, that I must tell it all.

Very well, here is the rest of the story.

After I graduated from high school and went off to college, I went on well for the Lord for a few months before I fell into sin, joined the Navy, ran off to sea, and lived the life of a prodigal for seven years. The Lord recovered me, but He had to break me to do it. The ascent out of the pit was, for me, painful and slow and difficult. "What profit is there in telling this part of story?" someone might ask. If you will allow me to tell the story, then you can determine whether or not it was profitable.

Bob and Evon warned me, Ellie Wassom warned me, Jim McIntyre warned me, every one of my elders warned me, that college was not an easy experience for a Christian to live through without having his faith badly shaken. They cautioned me, and I went blithely off to college without the least concern for my future. After all, I was Doug Miller, indomitable, a leader of men, a spiritual giant. I was none of these things, except for being Doug Miller, and it wasn't long before I was in trouble up to my eyeballs. The particulars of my failure are mine and mine alone, and they will not necessarily conform to those of the guy next door or the lady across the street. But the generalities—principles abstracted from the particulars—are universally applicable and ought to be heeded. The enemy is not infinite after all, and he has a bag of tricks with only a few items in it, items that he drags out and uses over and over because they have served him well over the millennia. I have had many years to think about my failure, and what follows is what I have concluded.

I took a philosophy course in college. I had always been fascinated by the philosophers, and I wanted to find out what these guys were all about. In the class we discussed, among other things, a Seventeenth Century Italian from Pisa whose name was Galileo. This man's problems with the Church troubled me greatly. His problems with those quoting the Bible to him troubled me even more.

Galileo took up the challenge of delineating the Solar System from a Polish astronomer, Copernicus, and pushed things much farther than the Pole had ever dared. Copernicus had not actually said that the earth revolved around the sun; he merely noted that matters would be easier to explain and to understand if we allow the sun to be the central point of reference. The Pope and the learned doctors of theology in Rome saw the implications of this and immediately moved to put the quietus to Copernicus's aberrant teaching. Copernicus died before they could get their hands on him. Galileo was not so lucky.

He not only stated that the sun is fixed, and that the earth is one of several planets moving around it; he went on to demonstrate that the law of falling bodies as Aristotle had formulated it is manifestly false. He proceeded to get deeper into heresy by stating that "up" and "down" are useful concepts relative to the earth and our place on it, but that in the cosmic scheme of things they are meaningless. He was dragged up before an ecclesiastical court, made to recant and branded a heretic, a charge that stood for three hundred years. Pope John Paul II finally dropped it.

Galileo was right, of course, and the entire papal delegation was foolish. So, how did this start my descent into the maelstrom? Please pay close attention.

I had no difficulty acknowledging that Galileo had been right. Nor did I, a non-Catholic, have a desire to vindicate the pope and his cardinals. The problem for me was that those opposing Galileo made their case against him from Aristotle and from the Bible. Aristotle I could work my way around, for he was just an old Macedonian with some brilliant ideas and some that were goofy. The Bible was another matter.

If one wishes to argue against scientists or philosophers, and if one wishes to oppose them with the Bible, one must make very certain that his understanding of the Bible is the correct one. The ecclesiastical doctors threw Genesis chapter one at Galileo and said that his theory of the Solar System contradicted the plain statements of Holy Writ—*ergo*, he could not be correct. I have read Genesis many times, and I cannot imagine in what school of logic the learned clergymen matriculated. Obviously they held to a theological position, and they allowed that position to dictate to them what the Scriptures said. In fact, they held that, according to the account of creation, the earth was flat and the fixed center of the universe overarched by a great blue canopy called heaven. The sun, moon and stars were positioned on that canopy, and the whole thing revolved around the earth. Because the earth was flat and fixed, down was down and up was up—end of discussion.

For me, however, the discussion had only started, and this is where my descent into confusion began. If Galileo had stood against the papal authorities and the Bible, and if the Bible, as they understood it, had been wrong, then what else was wrong? As I have already noted, the Bible was not wrong. The priests and doctors held to a false interpretation of it. The eighteen-year-old I then was could not make that distinction. In short, I began to doubt the truth of the Word of God, and panic began to set in.

I went to older believers for counseling. They pointed me back to the Scriptures to prove the correctness of the Scriptures. This helped me not one iota! How can I know that the Bible is true? Because the Bible says that it is true. This circular reasoning (philosophers call it begging the question) proved nothing to me. My elders didn't understand my confusion, and matters grew worse.

I now ask what they should have done, what they might have done. It is difficult to pass judgment on these decent people who loved me greatly, but I must, not to justify myself but to help someone else living through such a trial, or to help those trying to help a similarly afflicted soul. They ought to have taken the Book up and shown me its internal consistency, how it all fits together and moves from beginning to conclusion without contradiction. Or, they might have taken the many prophecies that have been so literally and completely fulfilled. I needed a good and godly apologist. I found none. My dear friends meant well, but they were unequipped to handle a young man walking through a vale of bewilderment.

Step two of my descent awaited the tread of my faltering foot. I began to feel guilty about my doubts, and no matter how often I confessed them as sin, the sense of guilt persisted and deepened. I began to wonder if all along I had been involved in nothing more than an exalted theological fairytale. Perhaps none of it was true.

In step three I could no longer tolerate being around Christians, particularly if those Christians had about them the aura of victory and joy and love for the Lord. Without realizing it, and because they had no idea of my spiritual struggle, they greeted me in the old ways, asked me to pray for them, told me about things they were learning from the Lord. They possessed the salt of the earth, they were the salt of the earth, and they unwittingly rubbed that salt into my open wounds with every word and gesture.

Step four approached with gathering momentum. It was becoming easier and easier to get farther and farther away from my Lord. In step four I started avoiding Christians all together. If I saw them coming, I ducked around a corner. If they invited me to a Bible study or a prayer meeting, I found excuses not to go.

And the guilt—the great, burdening, painful guilt—persisted.

Guilt is a terrible thing to live with. In fact, assuming one is half normal, guilt simply cannot be lived with. One will find, because he must find, a way to alleviate its unbearable weight. The correct way is to admit to the guilt, to confess it and forsake it; but when one is plagued with doubt about the truthfulness of God's Word, one can never have the assurance of forgiveness. "Jesus died for you," someone might say. "They lifted Him up on the bitter tree, and He poured out His life's blood to take away your sin and your guilt." Do any reading this comprehend how empty this proposition sounds to the individual who is not sure the Bible is true? The guilt hung on. I dealt with it in the only way I knew how, by telling myself I was an honest doubter and that those preaching to me about forgiveness were dishonest hypocrites.

Yes! That was it! I had finally hit upon the solution to my problem, and I began to feel much better about myself. Who needed to go through life a whimpering neurotic when he could blame all his problems on other people and infantile, unexamined beliefs? I would line myself up with Hegel and Nietzsche, and with all those heroic philosophers who stood face up to the gales of life without the necessity of crutches and props. I would be an honest unbeliever.

It worked for a while, then the guilt crept back in. So I ran. I had to get away from the believers whose very love and concern drove me to delirium. I had to get away from the burning, all-seeing eyes of an infinite, omniscient God. I did what men have been doing ever since the days of Jonah. I joined the Navy and went off to sea, off in the direction of my personal Tarshish, off to the ends of the earth where ships topple over into the abyss and are never seen. The sailors wouldn't care that I was a man running from God, and I would be at peace, rocked into slumber by the rolling sea.

Wouldn't you know it? One of the first men I met at boot camp was a born-again believer living for the Lord Jesus and willing to stand up and testify for Him. He was even a former Young Life club member. To make matters worse, he knew Jim McIntyre—or he at least knew who he was. I couldn't seem to get away from these characters.

Suffice it to say that my rebellion did not continue. The Lord, who began the work in me, is performing it and will perform it until the Day of Jesus Christ. Had He not recovered me and brought me back, I would not be sitting here at this time writing these words. The recovery was slow and painful, and it began with my admitting that I had been wrong, that the Lord was the righteous one and that I had behaved like a fool. I suppose I could compose a book about my restoration, but I am not sure it would be very edifying, and I am very sure it would be out of place in this story. God rescued me. For my present purposes, that is all anyone needs to know.

Now, back to Putnam City. What was going on back there while I was gadding about making a fool of myself? Did my fall into sin put everything there on hold and bring the work to a halt? It did nothing of the sort. This was as good a way as any for me to learn the humbling lesson of just how dispensable anyone is when the Lord is doing a work. The loss was mine. The prayer meeting at Putnam City went on, and on, and on. Well into 1961, four years after we started it, kids were coming out, and lives were being changed. The Lord raised up others to take my place. To the very end the meetings never had a name, never took on any official trappings, never had the sanction of any organized denomination or Christian group, and never had any adult supervision.

I don't know what finally brought the meetings to an end. When I returned to the Putnam City area, over seven years later, they had stopped. What remained were hundreds of people whose lives had been touched by God and who would never again be the same.

20

We all have to die.
~ John Garfield in *Body and Soul* ~

I'll shout with thy likeness
Impressed on my brow
If ever I loved thee,
My Jesus, 'tis now.
~ William R. Featherstone ~

Oh the love that drew salvation's plan!
Oh the grace that brought it down to man!
Oh the mighty gulf that God did span—
At Calvary.
~ William R. Newell ~

A question must inevitably follow: Was all of this real? I answer, it was real all right. I know, for I lived it. The questioner might be quick to say that he or she is not asking if the events actually took place but whether there was any depth to the reported conversions. Emotions run high in most humans, but in none so much as in teenagers full to overflowing with hormones and youthful energy. It's all so predictable. Get the kids together in crowded rooms where individuality is lost and mob psychology reigns. Get them all stirred up by singing and appealing to their hearts rather than their heads. Raise the powerful specter of Jesus before their bewildered eyes and talk to them of eternal life. Reduce them to tears with words like "love" and "beauty." Paint a picture for them of a world than can exist only in dreams.

Much as the more cynical among us would like to believe that this is what happened, I am here to testify that most of those I knew back then are going on for the Lord Jesus Christ today, and that what may have begun as nothing more than an emotional reaction to the Gospel message struck deep into their hearts and became a conviction that will carry them into eternity. Almost all will admit to having had their ups and downs. Some washed out at some point and doubted the reality of their salvation and the truth of what they had said they believed. Some fell away and never came back. Some never had a real commitment to the Lord, they were only going along with the crowd because, for reasons none can clearly explain, all the exciting school action centered in on the prayer meetings and the Bible studies.

But most went on.

Most of these went on for the Lord as what the world is pleased to call laymen and laywomen. This clergy-laity business makes me tired. As Martin Luther aptly pointed out many years ago, there is no such thing as a holy calling for some believers and a less holy calling for others. All believers are in a full-time calling no matter what their chosen line of work may be. A Christian ditch-digger is what he is where he is because that is where the Lord has put him. With every spade of dirt he turns over, he is glorifying the Lord, and he is a God-anointed evangelist to every person he encounters. Yes, the prayer meeting spawned a few preachers, several full-time youth workers, even a missionary or two. The rest did other things.

Mike Davis was a stockbroker for a while, ran a restaurant for a while, then sold insurance. He has also traveled the world handing out Bibles for the Gideons, and today he has two Bible studies meeting weekly in his home.

Nancy McNatt became a mother and a housewife.

Connie Mason had sense enough to marry someone other than me, went to Florida, made big money in the real estate business and served the Lord where He had put her.

Bill Sam Knight became a maintenance employee in the high school of a rural community. This was the perfect place for him. He was not a preacher and never aspired to be one. But he had a great love for kids, a remarkable capacity for listening and speaking a word in due season and a beautiful, non-offensive way of pointing confused and troubled students to the Lord. He retired for awhile, then he went back to work part-time to be available, the Lord's man, giving out the Word whenever he can.

Alan Trimble became a psychiatrist.

Kenny McClain managed a large YMCA facility.

Joe Ed Tracy was an electrician.

Abby French taught mathematics in a junior high school.

Jack Holt got a B.S. degree in agriculture but never actually used it. He liked working with his hands, and he spent over forty years working as a carpenter, which is what he was doing when he first met Bob and Evon.

Bob Potter sold his grocery business in about 1960, and he and Evon went with the Navigators full time. Bob outlived Evon by several years. Both have now gone home to be with the Lord. Their funerals were held at Metropolitan Baptist Church in Oklahoma City, presided over by David Cotten before an auditorium filled to overflowing. People came for miles to honor this incredibly gifted and dedicated couple. Only in eternity will we know how many lives they touched.

David Cotten is alive and well as of this writing. I talk to him from time to time. He is no longer preaching, but for many years he taught a Sunday school class, which my daughter and son-in-law attended. He recently had to give it up. Ah, time! It gets us all. I will long remember that at Evon's funeral David closed by quoting Jude 25: "Now unto Him who is able to keep you from falling, and to present you faultless before the presence of His glory with exceeding joy." Bob and Evon are there.

Jim McIntyre gave up his job, went to a seminary and became a Presbyterian minister. One day, unexpectedly, he suffered a heart attack and fell dead in the living room of his home. Jim is there, at the Throne, faultless, with exceeding joy.

Ellie Wassom is there too. She went to Dallas as a youth director in a large church. The last time I saw her I drove to Dallas specifically for that purpose. She was simply beautiful, with that beauty of the soul and spirit that can come only to a godly woman given wholly to the Lord. We went to lunch together, laughed about the old times, talked about the amazing revival that we had seen sweep through Oklahoma City. Not long after that I got a letter from her telling me that she had cancer. It was malignant, inoperable, terminal. She spent her last days in a nursing home, and (Wouldn't you know it?) she got up a Bible study with a group of elderly, dying women. As long as she was able, she gave out the Good News of Jesus Christ to anyone she could get to listen.

I have long since lost touch with many of those who came out to the prayer meetings. But occasionally I run into one of them, often at funerals, sometimes at class reunions. We never have a reunion of the class of 1958 without one of our members, at some point, offering up a moving prayer of thanks to the Lord. "We were always different than the other classes," Kenny McClain told me. "There was a spiritual edge to us that you just don't see in many groups."

He was right.

The End